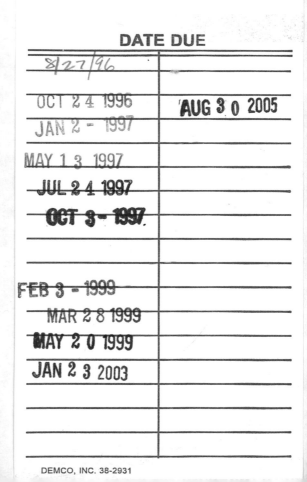

DATE DUE

8/27/96	
OCT 24 1996	AUG 3 0 2005
JAN 2 - 1997	
MAY 1 3 1997	
JUL 2 4 1997	
OCT 3 - 1997	
FEB 3 - 1999	
MAR 2 8 1999	
MAY 2 0 1999	
JAN 2 3 2003	

DEMCO, INC. 38-2931

Hugo Verlomme

TRAVEL BY CARGO SHIP

Cadogan Books plc
London House, Parkgate Road, London SW11 4NQ, UK

Distributed in North America by
The Globe Pequot Press
6 Business Park Road, PO Box 833, Old Saybrook,
Connecticut 06475–0833, USA

First published as *Le Guide des Voyages en Cargo*
by J.C. Lattès, Paris, © Hugo Verlomme 1993, 1994

UK copyright © Hugo Verlomme 1995

Book and cover design by Animage
Cover illustrations by Andrew Lovell
Maps © Cadogan Guides, created by Animage

Series Editors: Rachel Fielding and Vicki Ingle

Translated by Dominique Shead and Nicola Gadsby
Editing and proofreading: Dominique Shead
Indexing: Dominique Shead and Toby Bourne
Macintosh: Jacqueline Lewin
Production: Rupert Wheeler Book Production Services

ISBN 0-86-0110-355

A catalogue record for this book is available from the British Library

US Library of Congress Cataloging-in-Publication Data available

Output, printed and bound in Finland by Werner Söderström oy.

To travel hopefully is a better thing than to arrive.

Robert Louis Stevenson

About the Author

Hugo Verlomme is a French scriptwriter, novelist and writer about the sea. He has travelled in the northern hemisphere on various ships, liners and cargo vessels.

Acknowledgements

The publishers would particularly like to thank John Alton at Strand Cruise & Travel Centre for all his help. Also thanks to Animage, Nicola Gadsby and Jacqueline Lewin.

Note: The author and publishers have made every effort to ensure the accuracy of the information in the book at the time of going to press. However, they cannot accept any responsibility for any loss, injury or inconvenience resulting from the use of information contained in this guide.

Contents

Introduction

The publication of this guidebook in France in 1993 was a first. Until then, only a small circle of people in the know were privy to the ins and outs of travel by cargo ship. Now these facts are available to everyone.

The popularity of this book has clearly demonstrated that demand for this mode of travel is increasing. Travellers, sailors, artists, lovers of the sea, retired people and wanderers—more and more people are seeking to travel by sea, in Europe and in America: this guidebook has been translated into German and Italian, as well as English.

In the UK, Germany and USA the cargo ship market is growing, with numerous specialized agencies and new shipping companies accepting passengers on board. This book offers dozens of trips, long and short, from the luxurious to the most economical.

The fact that increasing numbers of people are expressing their wish to travel by cargo ship has dictated what happens in practice, and we can only hope that more and more shipping companies will begin to accept passengers. Thinking of the number of empty cabins on working cargo ships gives us hope for a rosy future ahead.

So happy reading and, above all, *bon voyage*!

The Romance of the Sea

Travelling by sea… a dream as old as humanity itself.

Not so very long ago the ship was still the only means of setting out to discover new horizons. The very first sailors and pirates who set sail into uncharted waters were without doubt, according to Buckminster Fuller in his *Instruction Manual for Spaceship Earth*, the first men with a sense of planetary consciousness. (Architect, engineer, philosopher and visionary, the American Buckminster Fuller (1895–1983) was the inventor of the geodesic dome and one of the fathers of planetary consciousness).

> *The further they travelled during their maritime adventures, the more they realized that the water was a real link between all the peoples and regions of the world. But no-one, apart from them, knew this.*

Nowadays, the dominating position of the aeroplane has all but obliterated the concept of sea voyages.

So is it still possible to travel by sea today? The answer is yes—you can buy tickets for cargo ships (or freighters, as they are known in the United States) which sail all over the world. This method of transport is becoming increasingly popular and there is no lack of ships. In fact, it is worth knowing that 98 per cent of world trade is transported by ship! This remarkable figure does much to set the record straight. There are about 40,000 cargo ships scattered all over the world, and many of them sail with empty cabins in which they could carry passengers.

Since the beginning of the 1990s travel by cargo ship has seen a real revival. This benefits everyone: passengers and shipping companies, and also the officers on board the ships, the vast majority of whom enjoy having travellers on board.

Cargo Blues

Travel by cargo ship conjures up a host of literary and historic images, dominated by a few major figures.

The first of these is, of course, Joseph Conrad, one of the greatest 20th-century novelists, who was of Polish origin—his real name was Jozef Konrad Korzeniowski. Orphaned at the age of ten, he enrolled in the French merchant navy in Marseilles and later joined the British Royal Navy. For Conrad, the sea represented a constant search for new experiences and served as the inspiration for his magnificent novels.

Malcolm Lowry, author of *Under the Volcano*, was also captivated by the sea and read Conrad a great deal. When he was 18 he worked as a deck-hand on a cargo ship en route for Japan. This voyage inspired his first book, *Ultramarine* (1933):

> *He went to the rails, which vibrated as though they would uproot them-selves from the deck. Fourteen men in a forecastle. How swiftly, how*

incredibly swiftly they had become a community; almost, he thought, a world... World within world, sea within sea, void within void, the ultimate, the inescapable, the ninth circle. Great circle...

The French novelist and poet, Blaise Cendrars, embarked on the *Birma* during the winter of 1910, acting as an interpreter on a ship full of emigrants. It was his first Atlantic crossing: 'It was a very small cargo ship, nothing transatlantic about it, but a good little tub which held her own in the sea. We still suffered terribly from cold and hunger. It was overflowing with the poor from all corners of Asia.'

Cendrars had a memorable transatlantic crossing: the ship lost her propellor in the middle of a storm! He came back the following year on the *Volturno*, a rusty old cargo ship returning emigrants turned back at Ellis Island to Europe. Once again, Cendrars was protected by the gods: on her subsequent crossing, the ship went down with all hands.

Between 1924 and 1936 Cendrars crossed the Atlantic every year, heading for North and South America, the only passenger on board cargo ships whose captains he grew to know, or else on board famous liners like the *Formose*, the *Lutetia*, the *Wisconsin*, and, of course, the *Normandie*.

Then there is the Canadian Jack Kerouac, the itinerant 'road' writer, adventurer and father of the 'beat' generation, who called one of his first books *The Sea is My Brother*. Kerouac predicted the negative influence the aeroplane would have: 'The Jet Age is crucifying the hobo because how can he hop a freight jet?' He recalls in *Lonesome Traveler* his life as a kitchen-hand on a tramp steamer shuttling between the USA and Mexico in the 1950s, juxtaposing the hours spent in the depths of the galley with other more peaceful days:

> *Holy sunrises and holy sunsets in the Pacific with everybody on board quietly working or reading in their bunks, the booze all gone.—Calm days, which I'd open at dawn with a grapefruit cut in halves at the rail of the ship, and below me there they were, the smiling porpoises leaping and curlicueing in the wet gray air, sometimes in the powerful driving rains that made sea and rain the same. I wrote a haiku about it:*

> > *Useless, useless!*
> > *—Heavy rain driving*
> > *Into the sea!*

In 1957 Kerouac chose to travel to Europe as a passenger on board a Yugoslavian cargo ship and was caught up in a violent gust of wind which the sailors referred to as 'Boorapoosh', meaning 'North Wind'.

In the aftermath of the Second World War, liners and passenger cargo ships struggled to meet the huge demand for transport across the Atlantic. The wounds inflicted by the war were still glaringly obvious: displaced people, soldiers returning home, emigrants desperate to leave behind the nightmares of war, travellers, adventurers, businessmen, investors... all impatient to reach their destinations. Though liners travelled at faster and faster speeds to attract their clientele, passengers looking up from the deck were faced with the mocking glint of aeroplanes on high.

The aeroplane gained ground insidiously; the Tintin books drawn by Hergé demonstrate very clearly this shift from the ship to the aeroplane. In his early adventures, which took place before the war, Tintin always travelled aboard liners, and later on cargo ships (the *Sirius*, the *Karaboudjian*, etc.), but his later books are entirely dominated by the skies: Tintin flying to the moon in a blaze of glory, and later the victim of an aeroplane crash (*The Red Sea Sharks*). In the following book he flies to Nepal in search of Tchang, the victim of another crash in the Himalayas (*Tintin in Tibet*); his penultimate story is entitled *Flight 714*, and the final drawing of his last book, *Tintin and the Picaros*, shows an aeroplane taking off, as if it were carrying with it the soul of the artist.

Jet Set

The advent of civil aviation signalled the liners' demise: two generations later and the whole world was dashing around in jets. The magical aeroplane can reach any part of the world in a few hours. But to what end? Where do you draw the line between necessity and luxury? Even today, we travel greater and greater distances for less and less money. A weekend break in Bali... Lunch in Paris, dinner in Peking... The world at your fingertips... A self-service planet... In the exotic department, Thailand and Nepal are on special offer: try them today!

The aeroplane is a wonderful tool, but it has killed travel and prompted the rise of the return ticket: it has now become almost compulsory to possess an onward ticket in order to gain entry into certain countries.

Some people say that this golden age of the aeroplane is already waning. Aviation is going through an unprecedented crisis and the days of jumping on a plane at the drop of a hat may soon be over. The president of Air France, Bernard Attali, declared in 1993: 'The airline industry is facing the most serious crisis of its history. It has lost more money in the last three years than it made in 20 years.' It is even possible that the price of air tickets will be subject to hefty increases in the near future, which would put travel by cargo ship in a new light. Moreoover, many passengers are becoming increasingly jaundiced with the aeroplane, a stark and soulless means of transport. For them a voyage by cargo ship would be a pleasant interlude, reconciling them to the idea of travel itself.

Present-day Travel by Cargo Ship

The idea of a voyage by cargo ship may evoke the romantic image of a passenger paying his way by mopping the decks, or a modest cabin without a porthole costing next to nothing. Those days are long gone—a fact which is relished by some and regretted by others.

Today's cargo ships offer facilities which are on the whole comparable to those of modern hotels, with all mod cons. The cabins are often more luxurious than those on liners. A steward looks after your every comfort. On the majority of cargo ships, you will be accommodated in a double or single cabin with its own shower and WC. Ultra-sophisticated cargo ships have varnished wood decor, candlelit dinners with the officers, obligatory evening dress and all the ceremony of the good old days. In the luxurious 'suites' you will find a video recorder, fridge and mini-bar, as well as vast scuttles (large square portholes dear to Captain Haddock), with unbeatable views. Other vessels are more modestly equipped, but just as robust and welcoming, and offer the same sights and service at a lower price—not forgetting the passenger-cargo ships which are proper little liners.

On board you will find a sitting room, a video lounge, a bar, very often a small swimming pool, and sometimes a sauna, gymnasium or library. You will take your meals in the officers' dining room, in their company, looked after by a maitre d'. Included in the price of the ticket are breakfast, lunch and dinner. Some lines offer free wine during meals. (The C.G.M. even has wine from its own cellar, bottled by the company.)

Some cabins are better equipped than others, but there is no first or second class, which makes socializing easier and leads to a generally convivial atmosphere. Everyone is therefore 'in the same boat', particularly as the passengers are in constant contact with the officers and are able to follow the progress of the ship.

On a passenger-cargo liner, which can transport 200 passengers (or more), you will find similar facilities to those of liners: restaurant, discotheque, shops, sauna, library, hospital, as well as entertainment, festivities and games. Thus a voyage aboard a cargo ship can be in the most luxurious conditions: not only is it a floating hotel, a unique observatory on the sky and sea, but it also takes you smoothly to your destination!

This is why the question: 'Is it cheaper than a plane?' is not relevant—we only spend a few hours in a plane against several days aboard a cargo ship, where every need is catered for. The cargo ship is not only a means, it is an end in itself.

Ticket prices can range between US$20 and US$300 per day, the average being around US$100 a day.

So even at 100 dollars a day, a voyage by cargo ship remains a bargain, as the price covers every item in the daily budget: transport, the trip and a change of scenery. What hotel could offer a comfortable room on the sea, three meals a day, with the voyage itself thrown in, for that price?

Above all, of course, cargo ships are working vessels designed to carry freight. Operational restraints can cause departure and arrival times to deviate by a matter of days or even weeks, which naturally requires great flexibility on the part of passengers. One passenger, Robert Van de Wiele, en route for South America on a Polish Ocean Lines cargo ship, gives an example: 'I boarded the *Lodz II* on 11 January at Antwerp. The ship had arrived on the correct day, but we only set sail on the 14th, as persistent rain delayed the loading of the cargo: mainly sacks of flour bound for Guayaquil.'

In rare instances a destination port can be changed, or a new port of call added in the course of the voyage. These little uncertainties are part of the charm of travelling by cargo ship and merely add spice to the adventure.

There are some regular shipping lines, however, which do offer reliable timetables, depending on the weather. The more frequently the ship sails, the more accurate the timetable. For a round-the-world trip, for example, there can be a delay of up to 20 days.

Cargo Ship Addicts

It is striking to observe how the great majority of passengers travelling on board cargo ships are old hands who are repeating the experience. Cargo ship addicts are steadily increasing. Take for example the lively account of this woman, who has travelled on numerous ships and compares liners with cargo ships:

> The luxury liners are really only floating hotels with the corresponding social life and routines and I am sure they are magnificent, but have their passengers even had any real experience of being at sea? Been closely followed by a school of dolphins, or picked up flying fish as they landed on deck, or seen a whale spouting? They surely don't hear the gentle creak of timbers as we very leisurely drift along or hear sailors sing as they swab the decks in early morning!   (Quoted by Bank Line).

The deck of a cargo ship is much nearer to the surface of the water than that of a liner, because with her hold full of freight the majority of her hull is underwater. Cargo ships simply follow the laws of nature whereby in order to be stable a vessel must be well ballasted.

Travel for Travel's Sake

Forget the jet lag which can spoil your holiday: long voyages unfold naturally to the tranquil rhythm of the ship. You arrive at your destination rested and often sun-tanned. Time zones are gently crossed and the days pass without you even noticing. Some passenger-cargo liners still have celebrations when crossing the Equator.

As for the international date line, which crosses the Pacific down the middle from north to south, this takes on a whole new dimension at sea, as related by a passenger on the *Columbia Star*:

> *We were told to advance our watches an hour and retard our calendar a day, so we will enjoy March 20th all over again. This is the first time I've ever experienced the full, uncorrupted effect of crossing the date line. In the past it has always occurred in flight and one missed the full effect as it is either shortened or lengthened drastically by the compacted changes in time zones.*

On a boat, social barriers tend to dissolve: the very fact of being at sea brings people together. One traveller observed: 'On the quay, the boat seems enormous, but once at sea it becomes tiny.' For the crew, both sailors and officers, the presence of passengers helps break the routine.

Days follow the general pattern of sailing, punctuated by meals, meetings, time for reflection, ports of call and weather forecasts. The sighting of a whale, iceberg or a fishing boat in the middle of the ocean distinguish one day from another. It is the ideal time for reading, writing, meditating...

A voyage in a cargo ship is all these things and many more. At sea you will find yourself both somewhere and nowhere, beyond frontiers. It's the last space which still belongs to no-one. One of the great advantages of a cargo ship voyage is that it takes you right to the heart of a city: the port, always steeped in history, which you will look upon with different eyes after several days at sea.

Taking Time is Back in Fashion

That's all very well, you may say, but you still have to have enough time to travel by cargo ship. Time... the eternal contradiction of our society: those with money have no time, and vice versa. Perhaps this phenomenon is at last coming to an end.

When you have only 15 or 20 days of holiday, you want to make the most of them, and the aeroplane appears to be an instant way of shortening distances and stretching your holiday time.

However, according to the sociologist André Gorz, the end of the 20th century heralds the end of salaried society. In the face of the rising tide of unemployment, a new distribution of work—and thus of time—seems inevitable. This means, for the citizens of the 21st century, a new relationship with time: more leisure pursuits and a different philosophy of life which will quite easily accommodate sea voyages.

The Revival of Cargo Ships

When liners eventually stopped carrying passengers on their regular shipping lines in order to concentrate on cruises, cargo ships did not immediately take over. Post-war cargo ships transported articles of all shapes and sizes, and loading was a complex operation which could take up to several days, depending on the type of freight and available man-power. While loading was underway, other cargo ships would be waiting their turn at their moorings. Thus timetables and itineraries were highly inaccurate and it was not easy, under those conditions, to offer cabins to passengers.

Between 1960 and 1980, there were only a few shipping companies left offering accommodation on their cargo ships. At that time, anyone wanting to travel in this way had to find their way round the famous *ABC Shipping Guide* (*see* p.200), aimed mainly at travel agents. It contained timetables and fares for ferries, cruise liners and cargo ships all over the world. With these basic facts, you could then embark on an exacting series of phone calls and letters to obtain further information.

It seemed that this mode of travel was over for ever. However, towards the end of the 1980s, those shipping companies that had kept up passenger services noted that demand was growing. In Great Britain, Germany and the USA, companies specializing in cargo ship voyages started to flourish, and published increasingly tempting brochures. Now some voyages are booked years in advance, and new cargo ships are being designed to take passengers. Even brand new passenger-cargo liners (*see* p.24) are appearing, and this really seems to indicate a revival in sea voyages.

The Container Ships Revolution

During the 1980s the number of container ships increased. Some of these giants are called 'Overpanamax' as they are so wide they cannot go through the Panama canal!

Because this kind of transport is standardized on a worldwide scale, and thanks to new means of communication, cargo ships are able to keep to timetables and itineraries much more reliably and precisely than in the past—which enables them to offer regular services to passengers.

However, many sailors feel that container ships have lost touch with something of the essence of the merchant navy, an opinion reflected by the writer–traveller Gavin Young in his book *Slow Boats Home*, on board the *Chengtu*, leaving Hong Kong:

> *As the steward carried in steaks, the conversation turned to what I came to recognize as a familiar topic at sea—the dehumanizing of life at sea by*

containers, computerization, cost efficiency. Ships don't linger in port as they used to. Shore leave is minimal, perhaps merely time for a beer. Schedules are calculated in hours, not days.

Show Me Your Container and I'll Tell You Who You Are

For the anthropologist, container ships endlessly circling the globe represent a real cross-section of our merchant society. A fantastic selection of products is contained in the millions of metal boxes aboard these floating Ali Baba caves, and countries form unexpected links when exchanging their respective merchandise. In an article in France's *Le Monde* newspaper, Philippe Abalan gives a witty account of his voyage on the *Fort-Desaix*, a C.G.M. container banana carrier:

> *In the 1,500,000 'boxes' piled ten storeys high in the hold and on deck, she is taking to the French West Indies—Fort-de-France then Pointe-à-Pitre—a motley assortment to satisfy even the most iconoclastic barbarian ...bottled water, alfalfa, earthenware tiles, fruit and vegetables from the West, onions, garlic, lard, fresh meat, slaked lime, folded boxes, empty bottles, car parts, tyres, fine salt, mountains of white sugar and potatoes for the sodas and chips which are gradually replacing natural fruit juices and creole rice (air-conditioned McDonalds and Burger King having recently opened in Fort-de-France), pigs' tails, frozen foods, crash barriers for a motorway under construction, nail varnish for Caribbean princesses, a surprising case of smoke grenades (to ward off demonstrators at the airport?), 3 kilos of unknown but dangerous 'lespenephryle', solvents, polyester resin, aerosols, caustic cleaner...*

Tramp Steamers

Compared to modern, functional cargo ships, which can be precise to within minutes, tramp steamers often have no advance itinerary and can be sent anywhere in the world. They are the descendants of the old type of tramp steamer, as described by Alvaro Mutis in *The Tramp Steamer's Last Port of Call*, an entrancing novel of which the *Alcyon*, a rusty old cargo ship, is the hero:

> *There was, in this roaming wreck, a kind of witness to our destiny on earth... a warm affection and solidarity for the tramp steamer rose in me. I saw in him an unhappy brother, a kind of victim of people's neglect and greed, to which his obstinate reply was to continue tracing in all seas the lifeless wake of his suffering.*

Tramp steamers which accept travellers nowadays, however, are nothing like those old vessels on their last legs. They offer old-style comfort, to the delight of their fans.

The Cargo Ships of the Future

The cargo ships of the future, which are currently being designed, will be built for speed, such as the 'Techno Super Liner', a cargo ship prototype which moves on magnetic propulsion, without propellers, and would be capable of reaching speeds of 50 knots. In 1994 the Japanese passed the 50-knot (93kmh) hurdle and designed a cargo ship able to reach that speed while carrying 2000 tons of freight. This would leave only 62 hours between New York and London.

Since the beginning of 1990 type SL7 container ships have been in operation, capable of keeping to an average of 33 knots on transatlantic and transpacific crossings (they consume 625 tons of fuel per day). More and more fast ferries and coastal boats are being put into service, designed along the lines of the SWATH-type catamaran (Small Waterplane Area Twin Hull, with reduced floatation). The luxury liner, the *Radisson Diamond*, was based on this futuristic model.

Yet sea and speed are not a good combination: above a certain speed the water becomes as hard as concrete, forming unexpected hollows and bumps. The sea imposes its own rhythm, which is of course an integral part of the pleasure of a crossing. What is the point of being on a boat if you can't go out on deck to admire the ocean? Above 20 knots, the vessel's movements become harder, and the combination of the wind generated by the ship's speed and the normal sea breeze can make any excursions on deck most uncomfortable.

The pleasure in any crossing lies precisely in its length: nothing is hurried; you can gradually acclimatize yourself to the sea. Departure and arrival days should be deducted from the crossing time, because land is still too close. Between those two days, you stop counting the days... provided that the voyage is long enough.

There is a world of difference between crossing the Atlantic in five days on a liner as fast as the QE2, and spending eleven days aboard the Polish liner, the *Stefan Batory* (now docked), drifting at 15 knots between Tilbury and Montreal, having sailed round Newfoundland, and lazily navigated the Gulf of St Lawrence.

And in the future? How long will it take to cover the 3200 miles which separate London and New York on a fast cargo ship? Three days? Or will we drift gently, silently, on ultra-modern liners and cargo ships, propelled by sail?

Slow is Beautiful

We are taught to love and appreciate speed and rapidity, as if our only aim were to race as quickly as possible towards the end of our journey. The aeroplane blinds and deludes us; it steals time—we arrive before we have even left. It erodes the notion of space, deceives us with distances and evades the real beauty of travelling, which is the journey itself. 'Tourists don't know where they went. Travellers don't know where they're going,' wrote Paul Theroux, rowing among the islands of the Pacific in his small folding kayak.

The first ingredient of travel is a leisurely pace. The destination is only a dream: slow is beautiful. Etymologically, 'voyage' signifies 'path to follow', but we have confused the end with the means. These days travel kills travel. The world is ours. Maps have become catalogues, countries 'products'. The world is shrinking: they're selling the South at a knockdown price.

The Aeroplane, Source of Pollution

On an ecological level, any comparison between the aeroplane and the boat is weighted heavily against the former. As an example, a Paris–New York return flight burns as much oxygen in the atmosphere as the entire population of Paris during a whole year!

We use aeroplanes an enormous amount, and are slowly discovering their damaging effects: atmospheric and sound pollution, kerosene vapours, oxygen combustion, impact on the ozone layer, exposure of passengers and crew to cosmic rays, etc. The indirect impact of civil aviation is no less strong, as the aeroplane allows us to fly anywhere in a matter of hours. This accessibility has spelt the end for the ends of the earth, the last wild tribes, deserted lagoons and never-ending tundra. A charter flight lets us have them for a fistful of dollars; we just have time to take some photos and leave behind us a few urban germs in these last preserved enclaves.

Undoubtedly the aeroplane is also an invaluable tool which helps to save people's lives, put out fires, reunite families, transport mail and, with the help of journalists, witness faraway events. And it can even give those with limited time the opportunity to travel by cargo ship (undertaking the outward or return journey by plane).

But the aeroplane should not be permitted to force us to abandon other forms of transport: trains—every day more train tracks are being dismantled around the world—and boats, which lend themselves so easily to leisure and travelling.

There are very few people who fly from pure pleasure: nowadays two thirds of passengers travelling by air are tourists. But at what cost to the planet?

Aviation remains the form of transport which consumes the most energy. In 1989 total aviation emissions, divided exactly between civil and military aviation, were estimated at 2 or 3 million tons of NO_x, 166 million tons of CO_2 (13 per cent of carbonic gas emissions from the transport sector), and 223 million tons of water vapour, corresponding to the combustion of 212 billion litres of kerosene. These are very significant quantities, about a quarter of which are injected directly into the stratosphere, at between 9000 and 12,000 metres, given the average altitude of flights. Polluting agents can remain there for up to a year, and the *temperature of –30°C or –40°C leaves vapour trails visible well after the aeroplanes have passed. These trails, as well as emissions of nitrogen oxide, aggravate the greenhouse effect and damage the ozone layer.*

L'Air, a report published by the Swiss society for the protection of the environment, 1993.

During the course of a few years the aeroplane has established a monopoly, eclipsing the transport of passengers by sea. After the Second World War, in 1949, there were 1,005,000 passengers on the North Atlantic: 72 per cent of them were still travelling by sea, while 28 per cent were already flying. Liners and passenger-cargo liners still had some good days ahead of them, until the difficult years from 1970 to 1980.

Today there is hope that this trend will finally be reversed and the empty cargo ship cabins will be filled—even that main line passenger ships and passenger-cargo liners will be re-established. This is even more desirable when viewed in environmental terms: boats cause proportionately less pollution, as was stated in September 1991 in the EU report on maritime industry: 'Ships consume less energy per transported ton and are less harmful to the environment on noise and atmospheric pollution levels than any other means of transport.'

On the noise front, one could object that ships with propellers do cause high underwater noise pollution: sound actually reverberates three times as fast underwater as in the air, and it is feared that the throbbing of ships' motors, audible from a great distance underwater, has a negative impact on marine life, and more particularly on whales, who can communicate at great distances from one another.

'The Ship is Man'

Whales and dolphins are there to remind us, if we needed reminding, of our marine roots: the destiny of humanity is linked to the sea. Our planet, 71 per cent of which is covered with water, is a huge waterway, an open door on the whole world. One drop of water leads to the ocean: the sea is round.

Friedrich Ratzel, one of the founders of political geography, said in 1897: 'A country needs only a sea port to be capable of reaching any point in the far corners of the world. The sea is a route of communication which can lead everywhere.'

Following the explorers, warriors, traders and pro-slavers, other ships, full of pioneers, travelled the oceans to sow human seeds on new worlds. The common thread linking the *Mayflower* and the *Titanic* almost makes one forget the passing of the years. The first freight carried by boats with rounded maternal hulls is man himself: in turn explorer, shipwrecked, pirate, slave, then pioneer...

The ship is a parable of humanity. Or, as Victor Hugo wrote: 'The ship is man'.

Liners or Cruise Ships?

*After 1900, westbound transatlantic traffic grew phenomenally. Through-
out the 1840s, only 150,000 had crossed per annum; after 1905, over a
million a year made the same journey. It has been estimated that during
the century between 1820 and 1920, a staggering total of 34 million passengers crossed the Atlantic to America, preponderantly humble
emigrants yearning for a new life in the New World.*

These figures are recalled by one of the greatest liner specialists, the American
writer John Maxtone-Graham, author of the well-known *The Only Way to Cross*,
and more recently of *Crossing and Cruising*. Only a few years separate yesterday's
liners, filled with emigrants bound for Ellis Island, from the luxurious cruise ships
we see today.

Liners transported pioneers, refugees and travellers in search of adventure on this
transatlantic route. Some made the crossing in first-class luxury, while others were
squashed at the bottom of the hull, often in deplorable sanitary conditions, willing
to put up with anything in order to reach a new world full of promise and leave
behind them the horrors of the pogroms and other massacres.

The fact that this cargo-ship guide exists today is because liners no longer perform
the function for which they were built: transporting passengers from one point to
another. They gradually gave way to cruise liners, and for the first time travel
became an end in itself. Voyage by cargo ship has become practically the only way
of covering a long distance by sea.

Cargo ships and liners have a distinctive charm of their own and nowadays the
cruise boat industry keeps afloat a worldwide fleet of liners maintained in
working order.

The *Normandie*: the End of a Reign

In former times, liners served as ambassadors for their native countries; the
Normandie represented the climax of a great era and her arrival in New York in
1935 had an enormous impact. She was considered a 'masterpiece of French tech-
nology and art' and people even described her as the most beautiful and elegant
liner in the world.

Her inaugural voyage was memorable, with a glittering array of personalities on
board. Writers were invited to 'cover' the event; among them were Colette and
Blaise Cendrars, then a journalist on *Paris-Soir*, who had a different attitude from
other writers, as his daughter Miriam describes:

> *While others took as the theme of their article the sumptuous salons of
> the floating palace and the glittering life on board—black tie dinners,
> balls, concerts, shows, games, celebrities, high society, the sheer joy of*

doing nothing—Blaise, who still didn't possess a dinner jacket, went down into the hold and spent the four days, three hours and a few minutes of the record Atlantic crossing with the 1320 crew, whom no one else would have thought to address: the mechanics, the radiotele-graphers, all those who made this giant of the seas work—313m, 79,000 tons, 160,000 turbo-electric horsepower and 4 propellers—and thanks to whom the Normandie *won the Blue Ribband for its speed, comfort and luxury.*

Passengers on liners were very different from today's cruise ship passengers, motivated as they were by the concepts of departure and destination. This aspect inevitably heightened passions, and many fates were sealed aboard the liners of yesteryear.

The Last Transatlantic Ships

The 'war' against aeroplanes was lost. Liners gradually turned their attentions to cruise passengers. During the 1980s, because of a boycott by American dockers protesting against the Soviet invasion of Afghanistan, the liner *Aleksandr Pushkin* was unable to dock at New York. Following this incident, the Soviets in turn stopped transporting passengers across the North Atlantic. This left only two liners on the route, each very different from the other: Cunard's *Queen Elizabeth 2* and Polish Ocean Lines' *Stefan Batory*.

The QE2, using the transatlantic line as a cruising ground, became in 1993 the last remaining ship to use this legendary line (26 crossings a year, from April to December). The price of the ticket includes a return journey by plane, but there is also a return charter option available to those dedicated to travel by boat: passengers spend between 1 and 4 months in America and agree to return aboard the QE2 on a fixed date. The 1995 prices of a return ticket (both ways on QE2) range from £1595–£6765; with the return by aeroplane, £995–£5485.

The QE2 is very fast (32.5 knots!), and the joys of the voyage last a mere 5 days. As on all large liners, the crossing is enlivened by conferences, concerts, fine ballet performances, and other festivities. Celebrated chefs officiate in the kitchens, and the wine is served by genuine wine-waiters.

The *Stefan Batory*, a rather more modest vessel, was one of the last in a long line of transatlantic ships, boasting a lengthy history which has been described as 'lucky': an old-style liner, full of charm, which linked Europe and Canada by way of the magnificent Gulf of St Lawrence. She succeeded the *Batory*, which was one of the first ships to offer tourist cruises in 1953 (to the North Cape).

At the end of the 1980s the *Stefan Batory* had to put a stop to her crossings, and tried her hand at cruises—the Caribbean in winter and the Mediterranean in summer. Old and outdated, she was sold to a Greek shipowner in 1988. Other liners have been converted into hotels, such as the *Enchanted Isle*, which became the Commodore Hotel in St Petersburg, making up for the lack of accommodation in a city full to the brim with tourists.

Six Million Passengers

While so many companies struggle through the recession, the cruise industry has never looked so healthy, particularly in the USA, which held 80 per cent of the world market in 1992, with 1500 agencies specializing in cruises and 4.4 million passengers during a single year, compared with 665,000 in Europe and 250,000 in the rest of the world.

In 1993 there were roughly 200 passenger liners operating around the world. The cruise industry was worth £4.8 million and the market had risen steadily by 10 per cent a year since 1970! The stated aim was to reach 8 million passengers by the year 2000.

Since emerging land accounts for only 29 per cent of the world, cruise liners can cover two thirds of the planet for their customers. The Caribbean remains the most popular destination, within a plane's reach for Americans, who are fond of fun cruises in the islands. During 1993, 3.2 million cruise passengers transited through Miami alone.

This expanding market invents new 'products' each year to cater for an increasingly demanding clientele, and a good number of these liners resemble floating casinos. A company called Celebrity Cruises offers 'cyber-cruises' on board liners whose cabins are equipped with virtual-reality computers, allowing two passengers to meet in virtual reality before encountering each other face to face.

Cruise ships can provide access to out-of-the-way areas which are too inaccessible for the tourist market, becoming real floating hotels, like the Paquet company's *Ocean Princess*. This liner is moored at Paradise Bay in the Antarctic and enables tourists to visit remote places in luxurious conditions.

Cultural Cruises and New Concepts

Cruises are often designed around a theme, based for example around the ports of call. Theme cruises—a speciality which the Paquet company claims it invented with its 1956 musical cruise—are becoming increasingly common: 'Lyrical Cruise', 'Faces of the World, a Report', 'Opera and Operetta'. More educational themes can be adopted, such as 'Colonial History', taken in the company of lecturers, or else cruises organized around a particular event, like the 'Cinema Centenary Cruise' in 1995, run by Paquet and Pathé Cinema.

A ship at sea certainly provides a unique environment for listening to concerts or conferences, seeing films, and even undertaking group work, and a floating university in the USA, accommodated on liners, is a reflection of this concept. Founded in 1963, this 'University of the Seven Seas' demonstrates the potential usefulness of outdated liners, having enrolled over 20,000 students, who have discovered more than 60 countries. Since 1971, the *Universe* has travelled round the world with 500 students and professors from different universities and countries, holding seminars pertinent to their field of study. This really does put outdated liners to good use. These university cruises are open to 'non-student' passengers as well, who can also follow courses, workshops and seminars. (Institute for Shipboard Education, University of Pittsburg, 811 William Pitt Union, Pittsburg, PA 15260, USA.)

Cruises can also offer the ideal opportunity to improve your mind and meet people. In its brochure, the American cruise company Crystal Harmony boasts:

> *the most extensive lecture and seminar series at sea. The program is offered in an assortment of the ship's lounges including Club 2100, the Galaxy Lounge, the Palm Court and the Hollywood Theatre. Speakers range from high-level ambassadors and foreign diplomats to guest chefs and renowned wine connoisseurs. The program also features destination-oriented historians, popular authors and television journalists as well as top-name movie celebrities and noted business and financial leaders.*

In the case of long ocean-going crossings with no ports of call, such as a transatlantic crossing, you can enjoy 'sport and health' or 'gourmet' cruises, as on the *Berlin*, owned by the Germany company Peter Deilmann.

Today's liners are built like luxury hotels out of some science fiction scenario: transparent domes, floating platforms deployed on the sea at ports of call to enable passengers to practise nautical sports, and light, spacious cabins. Everything on board is designed around pleasure and leisure: swimming pools, saunas, cinemas, theatres, concerts, conference rooms, casinos, ballrooms, nightclubs, restaurants, shops, jogging tracks, golf greens (!) etc. For those businessmen wary of being cut off from their offices, there are rooms equipped with telephones, faxes and computers linked by satellite on the IMMARSAT system.

In an effort to attract a more family-orientated clientele, the Paquet company offers free trips to people under 16 accompanied by their parents or grandparents during term-time. Thus the *Mermoz* has a Junior Club with numerous activities for children (arts and crafts, games, films, shows, parties).

Sometimes these vessels hold serious conferences or seminars, since conditions on board ship are highly conducive to efficient working; these are 'incentive cruises', which are becoming increasingly popular. They allow a company to launch a new product, or improve its customer relations, as practised in the Mediterranean on board the Grimaldi company's *Ausonia*, a liner which—like many others—has its own conference centre.

In order to attract new, more demanding customers (in Europe, for example), companies have created the 'green concept'. Eco-liners include the astonishing, futuristic *Radisson Diamond*, conceived along the lines of a vast catamaran with reduced floatation, or the *Sovereign of the Sea*, which apparently does not discharge waste into either the water or the atmosphere, recycles its tins and even has a huge open-air garden! Today's liners have large panoramic seating areas, like those on the Royal Caribbean Cruise Line, which allow passengers to observe marine scenery through vast glass windows.

Shipowners build ever more enormous liners: the American company Carnival Cruise has ordered from Italy a giant of 95,000 tons at a cost of $400 million, which will accommodate 3400 passengers.

Using Liners as a Means of Transport

It's easy to forget that liners were originally built for carrying passengers and not for luxury holidays. Their original function has been eroded to such an extent that a cruise today generally involves one or two plane journeys, and it has become almost impossible to use liners as a means of transport.

Almost—the golden rule, if you want to travel the world in different boats, is that as long as there is a free cabin, there is hope! You are perfectly entitled to make enquiries at maritime and port agencies to find out if there is a cabin available on the vessel that interests you, and attempt to buy a ticket, even on a cruise ship.

The best illustration of this can be found in two books written by the travel writer Gavin Young, who relates with humorous realism his extraordinary round-the-world voyage on board the motley collection of boats which he encounters along the way (33 rusty old tubs, coasters, cargo ships, liners, etc. from Piraeus to Canton). The first volume, *Slow Boats to China* (1981), has already become a classic of maritime literature.

Gavin Young's tales demonstrate that with determination and some resourcefulness most obstacles can be overcome and the majority of passing boats boarded, including liners in the middle of cruises. After all, this is in the interest of the shipowner as well as that of the traveller. Gavin Young managed to secure a cabin from Papeete to Callao on board the Russian liner *Pushkin*, on a round-the-world cruise, and found himself in a comical situation: the only (English) traveller among hundreds of elderly German passengers, regarding him with extreme suspicion.

The author of this book has himself experienced something similar, when travelling from Hong Kong to Yokohama on a cruise ship in the company of the staff of a Japanese company studying wine...

Positioning Cruises

One original way of making a crossing in a cruise liner is by joining a 'positioning cruise'. Take the example of a ship based in Europe which cruises in the Caribbean in the winter, and in the Mediterranean in the summer. Between the two seasons, it has to make a transatlantic crossing to change areas, and this can be your chance to use the liner, as some companies sell cut-price tickets for these crossings. The number of passengers therefore depends on how many people are in the know. The ships are not usually full and sail without the multiple attractions of a cruise ship, in the style of the passenger liners of old. Positioning cruises are also undertaken when boats sail from their home base to their cruising area, or vice versa.

Fred and Marilyn, a New York couple who have made numerous transatlantic crossings aboard liners, experienced an unforgettable positioning voyage in the company of a small number of people, aboard the *Norway*. The passengers were inconvenienced by a few plumbing problems after departure, and the captain opened the bar for free drinks for the whole of the crossing by way of compensation!

Such events are rare, however: sea voyages have become so successful that more and more liners price their ocean crossings as full-tariff cruises; even so, they are still not as expensive as island cruises.

If you want to make a cruise-crossing without doing one part of the journey by plane, you can have an 'air-credit' deducted from the price of your ticket. A company called Costa, for its part, offers long transatlantic crossings in the autumn and spring, departing from Nice for Rio or vice-versa (four voyages a year). As an example, a ticket for the *Eugenio Costa* includes the air/sea combination, but a ticket excluding the plane ('port/port') is also available. The price for this 15-day crossing with ports of call in the Canaries, Africa and Brazil is 8645F (approximately £1000/$700) port/port—or 576F (£70/$45) per day—a fairly low price (comparable to cargo ship prices) for this type of voyage aboard a ship of this quality. There is a '3rd or 4th couchette' option for groups of 3 or 4 people, which allows the third or fourth adult to pay only 4960F (approximately £600/$400), or 330F (£40/$25) per day. On luxury cruise ships during high season, the price of the cheapest cabins can range from $250 to $600 per day, but they remain very popular: cruise ships have the highest number of repeat bookings in the whole travel industry.

Cargo ships, liners—vessels are always around: thousands of them ply the seas constantly. The demand for sea voyages is growing, and at least the cruise industry enables a fleet of liners to be maintained.

For many travellers, the transatlantic crossing remains *the* crossing. It would be nice to imagine, in the near future, a growth in traffic on this line, for at least six months of the year.

Who knows, perhaps these lords of the seas will one day go back to performing their original role of transporting passengers—history sometimes takes surprising turns.

Useful Addresses

Costa-Paquet: ✆ (0171) 723 5557, ✉ (0171) 402 0490.

Cunard: South Western House, Canute Road, Southampton SO14 3NR, ✆ (01703) 71600.

Different Passenger-cargo Ships

In the early days of the merchant navy, a cargo ship was by definition a hull into which was piled assorted merchandise: boxes, fresh produce, sacks, wood, animals, raw materials, etc. During the Second World War, German and Japanese submarines inflicted such heavy losses on Allied fleets that the USA launched an unprecedented programme of cargo ship construction. The boats were called 'Liberty Ships' and were multi-purpose cargo vessels, suitable for the transport of both troops and provisions. Built on an assembly line, some of them were put together in less than a week! Three years of frenetic activity at American naval shipyards saw the construction of at least 2700 Liberty ships. After the war, these multi-purpose cargo ships were redistributed to those countries worst affected by the conflict and played a key role in the reconstruction of Europe, constituting from the outset a formidable merchant navy fleet which could accommodate freight or passengers.

These days, however, multi-purpose cargo ships are rare: vessels have become more and more specialized and are built to suit a particular type of freight.

Container Ships

The container is a large metal case of 6–12m in length, and 2.44m in height, the dimensions being standardized on a worldwide scale. This standardization means that, whatever their respective country of origin, containers can be piled one on top of the other and can hold either dry or liquid goods (tank containers) or frozen matter (containers with their own refrigeration system and integrated generator). The entire chain of transport—crane, truck, train—is built around them and is identical all over the world, ensuring maximum 'door-to-door' efficiency and minimum handling. In 1992 there were 4.4 million of these containers in circulation. A series of giants capable of carrying 5000 to 6000 containers is being built for the end of this century.

Because of their reliability, container ships are often made available to passengers. They can be huge vessels and are expensive to build; for this reason they usually belong to a consortium of shipping companies.

In *Looking for a Ship*, the writer John Mac Phee recalls a voyage on board a container ship. Having arrived at Valparaiso, he makes a surrealist inventory of the freight:

> *We have a container of synthetic skin for sausages, water filters, automobile spare parts and another container of spare parts for lifts, for paper machines, for aeroplanes, neon lights, valves, plastic film, catalysts; 6.5 tons of sunflower seeds, 12.5 tons of alfalfa seeds, 364 boxes of hypodermic needles loaded in Colombia, 116 tons of laminated steel and 9 tons of copper wire (this even though we were in Chile!); 1.5 tons of ticket machines, 43 tons of used clothes, a crane model number 10880 and a fire extinguisher, amongst other things. We took on board 3000 crates of wine, 2 tons of short-sleeved shirts, 175 kilos of glue from*

Chilean fish and 113,000lbs of sugar; 817 desks and 817 chairs, 95 crates of umbrellas (bound for Los Angeles), 7000 retreads (for New Orleans), 6480 WC pans (Chicago). We are also carrying 9 tons of fruit juice cocktails, 63 tons of peach slices, 67 tons of raisins, 230,000 gallons of concentrated apple juice, 400,000 fresh lemons, 400,000 fresh onions, 500,000 fresh potatoes—then, finally, we cast off.

More often than not seamen have no idea what is in the containers, which they view as anonymous freight whose loading is controlled in advance by computer.

Roll-on Roll-off Container Ships

Roll-on roll-off container ships—or ro-ro's—have a deck very low above the water, which enables them to load cars and trucks by simple rolling—hence their name. Their most widely used application is car ferries, which load vehicles and passengers on ramps specially laid out for them on the quay. The classic freight ro-ro loads its containers using motorized vehicles. The advantage of the ro-ro is that she can operate in ports which are not equipped for containers (which require a special crane); she can simply dock alongside a quay, put down her ramp and load speedily and independently. A car carrier loads a large number of vehicles onto multiple decks, which can give her the appearance of a rather unlovely floating building.

Ro-ro's are generally used for short distances—in the Mediterranean or the North Sea, for example. The French company SNCM have two ro-ro's in service shuttling between Corsica, Sardinia and France: the *Porto-Cardo* and the *Kalliste* (carrying up to 190 passengers), which revive the old tradition of cargo liners. Some ro-ro's cover longer distances, such as the large car carriers owned by the Italian company Grimaldi, proper passenger-cargo liners which transport new cars and passengers between the Mediterranean, West Africa and Brazil.

Refrigerated Ships

These are cargo ships which specialize in the transport of fresh produce (fruit, meat, fish, dairy products), mainly between Europe and the Caribbean. Generally elegant and fast, capable of sailing at more than 20 knots, they are painted white in the tradition of the banana boat. On these top-of-the-range cargo ships it is quite common for each crew member to have his own cabin, and the facilities offered to passengers are fairly luxurious. Produce is carried in refrigerated compartments, whose temperature ranges from −30° to +12°.

Bulk Carriers

These vessels are built to carry non-packaged freight in solid or liquid bulk. Solid bulk includes, for example, iron ore, coal, cereals, phosphates, salt, etc., while liquid bulk covers petrol, bitumen, kerosene, liquid gas, ammonia, etc.

These ships are very attractive to travellers as they spend the longest amount of time at ports of call because bulk freight takes longer to load than containers or cars. It goes without saying that carriers transporting dangerous goods such as gas, petrol and chemical products do not accept passengers.

Tramp Steamers

Tramp steamers do not follow a regular route, as their itinerary depends on freight demand, and their destination can change in mid-course. As soon as a tramp steamer accepts a contract, it makes known its itinerary; since this may be two months in advance, or at the last minute, the passenger needs to be highly flexible. These ships offer the same degree of comfort as others, but at lower prices. You should ask companies who run tramp steamers, such as Egon Oldendorff or Mineral Shipping, for the 'position list' of their ships to see if there is an itinerary which suits your needs.

Passenger-cargo Liners

Passenger-cargo liners are the best compromise between cargo ships and liners. They allow over 12 passengers to travel aboard, which implies the presence of a doctor. Vessels currently operating are: the *St Helena* (between Great Britain and South Africa), the luxurious *Americana* (between the east coast of the USA and South America), the *Aranui* (in Polynesia), the *Kananga* (between Europe and Zaire) and the *Repubblica* series (between the Mediterranean and Brazil).

Ferries (or Transporters)

In order to compete with other forms of transport, a new generation of ferries is emerging which look more and more like liners. The former luxury ferry *Olympia*, for example, now *Pride of Bilbao*, has been chartered by P & O to operate two round trips per week between Great Britain and Spain (Portsmouth–Bilbao). In high season this 28-hour crossing is very popular: it enables the British to travel straight to Spain, avoiding the long drive through France. (Brittany Ferries operate a similar route twice a week between Plymouth and Santander.) This ferry, which can hold up to 2500 passengers and 600 cars, is the largest in Europe (37,500 tons) and offers saunas, a swimming pool, duty-free shop, nightclub and casino. Out of season she plys the Portsmouth–Cherbourg route.

In the Mediterranean ferry traffic is on the increase, and in 1994 there were over 50 ferries shuttling between Italy and Greece alone.

The largest ferry in the world operates between Helsinki (Finland) and Stockholm (Sweden). She is the *Silja Europa*, a luxury vessel able to accommodate 3013 passengers in 1194 cabins, which are equipped with telephones and colour TVs. On board there are seven restaurants, a 564-seat theatre, a 1000m sq supermarket and even—what decadence—the first floating McDonalds!

Planning Your Voyage

Introduction to the Practical Guide

Before launching yourself into the list of dream destinations in this guide, you will need to familiarize yourself with aspects of this kind of travel.

Some shipping companies carry passengers in only one specific area of the world (such as Safmarine in South Africa); others have cargo ships which go anywhere in the world; finally there are those (such as ABC Containerline and NSB) whose ships do non-stop round-the-world trips.

Agencies and companies always take great care to warn travellers of possible fluctuations in timetables and itineraries, in order to protect themselves against complaints. This is not to say that all cargo voyages are subject to these variations; on the contrary, some go exactly according to plan, down to the last minute.

As an example, here are the first words of a contract for a typical voyage between a passenger and a shipping company:

> *Bank Line vessels are working ships and their primary function is to carry cargo. Their departure dates, departure ports, ports of call and the duration of the passage may therefore be subject to wide variation, not only prior to the voyage but whilst en route.*

All documentation relating to passenger-cargo voyages carries this phrase: routes and fares are subject to change.

Even the ships mentioned in the brochure may be replaced by others at the last minute. Moreover, ships can change hands and be bought by other companies with surprising frequency.

Travelling from One Port to Another

There are many ways of going from A to B by sea, as illustrated by the example below, which details four different routes linking Rotterdam and Colombo.

Example: four ways of travelling from Rotterdam to Colombo.

1. One boat travels via France before heading south towards west Africa, South Africa and finally Cape Town and Sri Lanka.

    Rotterdam–Le Havre: 250 miles. Le Havre–Accra (Ghana): 3825 miles. Accra–Cape Town: 2592 miles. Cape Town–Colombo: 4395 miles.

    Total: 11,062 miles, i.e. about 28 days' sailing excluding ports of call.

2. The second boat goes via Gibraltar, the Suez Canal, the Red Sea, the Oman Sea, with ports of call in Greece, Saudi Arabia, the Persian Gulf and Pakistan.

Rotterdam–Piraeus: 2887 miles. Piraeus–Jeddah: 1320 miles.
Jeddah–Bahrein: 2428 miles. Bahrein–Karachi: 922 miles.
Karachi–Colombo: 1341 miles.

Total: 8898 miles, i.e. about 25 days' sailing excluding ports of call.

3.   A third boat, on an east–west round-the-world route, would reach
      Colombo by crossing the Atlantic via the United States, Panama, the south
      Pacific, Australia and Singapore. The round-the-world trip would be com-
      pleted via the Indian Ocean, stopping at Colombo, the Red Sea and the
      Mediterranean.

      Rotterdam–New Orleans: 4880 miles. New Orleans–Auckland: 7945
      miles. Auckland–Sydney: 1275 miles. Sydney–Singapore: 4275 miles.
      Singapore–Colombo: 1565 miles.

      Total: 18,375 miles, i.e. about 51 days' sailing excluding ports of call.

4.   The last boat might set sail straight for Colombo, non-stop, using the most
      direct route (the Suez Canal).

      Rotterdam–Colombo: 6785 miles, i.e. about 19 days' sailing.

The above example demonstrates clearly the fact that the basic 'Rotterdam–
Colombo' designation signifies very little without details of the ports of call, which
determine the route, the length of the voyage and, consequently, the price of the
ticket. This is why you must consider the price *per day*, and not in terms of the
actual distance between Rotterdam and Colombo.

Round Trip or Single Ticket?

The majority of vessels leave their home base, follow an itinerary and return. This
is called a round trip. It is more viable for a company or agency to sell round trips
like a cruise, which is why priority is given to passengers on round trips. They may
not necessarily wish to visit faraway countries but their aim is to spend several
weeks on board a cargo ship: the main point of the voyage for these people is the
ship itself. However, an increasing number of travellers wish to complete only one
part of a round trip, thus using the cargo ship as a means of transport rather than an
alternative to a cruise.

Inveterate drifters and devotees of single tickets should note that many countries
now insist on an onward air or boat ticket before granting entry. This means you
will have to make some outline preparations for your return trip. You do not necessarily have to return to your country of origin: your onward ticket could be for a
neighbouring country to the one in which you are travelling. Some immigration
services will issue an entry visa on the condition that you can guarantee them a
sum of money equivalent to the price of a return ticket on an escrow account.

The Ports of Call

In the past, cargo ships remained in port for days or even weeks, waiting for a space to dock or for manpower or merchandise, thus enabling passengers to visit the area.

The main complaint of cargo ship passengers today is the short amount of time spent at ports of call—sometimes only a few hours, as with some container ships or ro-ro's. Everything is geared towards the rapid loading and unloading of containers, and some container ships will only dock from 6 to 24 hours, though they may stay three days, depending on the country. Bulk carriers take longer to load, and Mineral Shipping tramp steamers dock for up to a week, enabling passengers to enjoy excursions ashore.

If you are travelling aboard a cargo ship with a regular itinerary, you could plan your voyage so that you stay ashore for the length of one rotation (a return journey) and leave with the following boat, thus spending more time in the port of call. A vessel will sometimes visit the same port twice during a single rotation, allowing you to plan a few days on shore while waiting for the second call.

The real experts sometimes opt for a trip during which the vessel has to be in dry dock for several days. A couple from Colorado, Polly and Bill Cullen, who have sailed on many cargo ships all over the world, decided to travel on the *American Senator* bound for South Korea, where the vessel was due to undergo repairs in dry dock. The length of the stopover was 3 weeks, allowing them to enjoy an unforgettable holiday in China.

Even the duration of the ports of call can be subject to last-minute alterations, as witnessed by an American traveller, Keith Comly, who arrived at Botany Bay port, Sydney, one Tuesday with his wife Jean aboard the container ship *Columbia Star*.

> *We were advised by the captain that we were scheduled to depart at 2300 hours... He did caution us, however, that delays may occur. One has to keep in mind the ship's priorities are cargo first and passengers second.*
>
> *On Thursday morning we were all reminded that our departure was still posted at 2200 hours and we must be back aboard no later than 2100 hours... At about 1700 hours we learned our departure had been rescheduled to 0600 hours the following morning. Most of us made it an early night as we felt compelled to be on the monkey bridge for our early departure. Unfortunately, we awoke early the next morning to learn our ETD [estimated time of departure] had been delayed another four hours. Normally you might think these delays would be frustrating. However, they added interest to our day. After all, we are in absolutely no rush to go anywhere and it is always interesting to watch the loading activities.*

One last point: in some towns the docks are several miles from the centre and you may have to call a taxi. Don't be late returning, as the ship may not wait for you if you are late!

Should You Improvise or Plan Ahead?

Some cargo ship voyages can be planned several months in advance, while others are organized at the last moment. With the help of this guide you will be able to decide which method suits you best.

If you wish to board a cargo ship without having prepared for your trip in advance, you should request information from large shipping companies which have numerous vessels operating all over the world, such as Polish Ocean Lines, Egon Oldendorff, Mediterranean Shipping Company, and Blue Star, or from specialist agencies (*see* p.199) able to confirm the whereabouts of their vessels.

One specialist American agency, Freighter World Cruises, has the following slogan: 'If you're not fussy about a destination, we can get you out on short notice.'

Why not decide that what is important is *how* you go rather than *where* you go? All the specialist agencies work with the large shipping companies whose boats visit western Europe before scattering to the four corners of the earth. In this frame of mind, you will always find a cabin on a departing cargo ship and the ship will determine your destination.

In all cases, you would be advised to make yourself available several days before departure. And even once you have your ticket in your hand, it is wise to ring the agent or the company three days before departure to confirm that the timetable is being adhered to.

The Cost of the Voyage and Money on Board

The price of tickets can fluctuate up or down and companies sometimes offer high or low season fares. Reduced fares may also be available if you embark at the last minute or during the stormy season. Port taxes are not always included in the price of the ticket; they vary between $40–$90 per voyage and per person.

With some companies and agencies it is obligatory for passengers to take out an insurance policy which covers them if the ship has to change its route in order to disembark them in case of serious illness. This costs between $80 and $140.

The price of the ticket includes all meals—breakfast, lunch, tea, dinner and sometimes drinks during meals—as well as the use of all passenger facilities.

On board, the only things that you will be able to purchase are drinks and cigarettes, usually duty-free, and a few inexpensive items from the ship's shop, payable in dollars or in the currency of the boat's home base.

There is a purser on board every passenger ship, who deals with administrative matters and the cash on board. He will be in charge of the safe in which you can place valuables, and you can ask him to send post for you at ports of call. Remember to take sufficient local currency with you for your ports of call, as you will not always be able to change money on board.

Any tips for cabin, restaurant and bar staff are at your discretion; the purser can advise you. For obvious reasons, don't leave it to the last day to give your tip and show your appreciation.

Age Limits and Medical Requirements

Different companies and ships have their own policies on minimum and maximum ages of passengers. Passenger-cargo ships often don't give an age limit because there is a doctor on board. On other cargo ships the minimum age is 5, as on the C.G.M. banana carriers; in rare cases it is 18, as on Harrison Line ships. Some companies accept children of all ages and even give them substantial discounts.

The upper age limit is usually 80 years of age. All passengers over 65 years of age must ask their doctor to complete a medical certificate stating that they are fit and able to travel. There are no doctors carried on board cargo ships, although one crew member usually has moderate medical qualifications in case of emergencies; however, it is essential that all passengers are in a state of good and stable health. Conditions which are unacceptable include:

1.   Any disability affecting full mobility. Passengers must be able to walk freely and unassisted and climb stairwell ladders. Use of wheelchairs, walking sticks and zimmer frames is not allowed.

2.   Any condition associated with dizziness, fainting episodes or lack of consciousness.

3.   Psychiatric illness.

4.   Unstable heart conditions, including angina.

Visas and Inoculations

Visas are often required and are compulsory at certain ports of call for all passengers travelling on a cargo ship. Unlike the airlines, the shipping companies are not part of the visa waiver scheme and therefore it is imperative that passengers obtain the required visas before embarking on their voyage. For example, a valid visa is required for visiting all US and Australian ports, even if the passenger does not disembark from the vessel.

Inoculations are also often required and compulsory when travelling on cargo vessels. All shipping companies and the specialized agents dealing with cargo ship voyages are able to provide details of all required visas and inoculations.

Insurance Cover

Insurance cover is compulsory for all passengers travelling on cargo vessels. A number of insurance companies do not provide adequate cover for travel on these vessels. However, specialized agencies offer very comprehensive cover which has been specially arranged for travel on cargo vessels.

Agencies and Companies

In order to buy your ticket, you should contact a shipping company direct, or else go to an agency. Some shipping companies have their own ticket office for passengers, others pass the work over to an agency. The ticket will be the same price whatever the source.

Specialist agencies exist in Europe, the United States and Canada, but Germany dominates the market. The largest usually represent 30 companies and offer several dozen voyages a year in their brochures. Most of these agencies also offer combined air/sea tickets, holidays and excursions on shore, etc.

Agencies include Hamburg-Süd and Frachtschiff-Touristik in Germany, the Strand Cruise and Travel Centre in London, Freighter World Cruises in California (which publishes its own newsletter twice a month) and Freighter Cruise Service in Montreal. In France a new agency called 'Mer et Voyages' opened in 1994.

Flexibility

Passenger-cargo vessels operate primarily for the carrying of freight and containers. Because of this dependence on cargo, they follow the pattern of international freight requirements which may vary from day to day. Consequently sailing schedules and itineraries are not always necessarily adhered to, unlike cruise ships.

It must be remembered that cargo vessels take time to load and discharge at ports of call and are prone to delay occasioned by weather, non-delivery of cargo and many other reasons.

Therefore, passengers must be flexible in their travel arrangements.

On Board a Cargo Ship

The Cabins

Most passenger cabins have the same facilities as officers' cabins and are much more spacious than liner cabins. They are well positioned, light and airy, and as comfortable as a good hotel room. A steward usually maintains them, depending on the shipping company and the vessel. Each cabin has armchairs, a table, chair, beds, almost always a private shower/WC, and sometimes a fridge and a video.

Most of the cabins have a scuttle (a large square porthole) with a view of the sea and are situated in the middle of the ship, well away from the noise of the engines. It is still advisable to check the position of your cabin, though, as some may have their views obstructed by containers.

If you want a cabin to yourself, you will probably have to pay a small supplement.

Food

On a ship, food assumes a much greater importance than on land. Mealtimes offer you relaxation and convivial conversation *par excellence*, a privileged chance to speak to the officers and hear their maritime anecdotes. On a cargo ship, you will be able to enjoy the facilities of a restaurant, eating as much as you like and not having to worry about the bill. The open air will make you hungry and the chefs make sure that nobody goes short!

In an old guide to cargo voyages, *Tramp Steamers, a Budget Guide to Ocean Travel*, the American journalist Meme Black gives her opinion on the dining rooms and the food:

> *What about the dining rooms? What about the food? Cheerful, modern and homey dining rooms—or saloons, as they are frequently called abroad—are situated on the highest deck to afford maximum light and view. As for the meals, food on freighters is notoriously delicious, with fresh-baked goods, succulent meats, and menus ranging from the national cuisine of the freighter line to familiar fare like pot roast.*

You may be surprised by the slightly Spartan timetable for meals, but you will quickly become accustomed to the timeless rhythm of the crew. At sea, time is divided up differently, especially when you are crossing time zones.

If you follow a particular diet (salt-free, vegetarian, etc.) let the company know: most will try to accommodate your needs, as long as you warn them several weeks in advance. With regard to alcohol served during meals, this varies from company to company. On some ships the wine is free, on others it is non-existent or you have to pay for it. It is a question of culture: you are more likely to find wine on a French or Italian vessel than a Polish one.

The Crew

One of the attractions of travelling by cargo ship is that as soon as you step on board you are transported to another world, coloured by the nationality of the officers and sailors. This is reflected in the language spoken, as well as in the food, the times of the meals and the customs.

These days it is increasingly common for officers and sailors on board the same vessel to be of different nationalities: British, German, American, Polish, Italian and Greek officers; Indian, Burmese, Malay, Filippino, Indonesian and Kenyan sailors, all on low salaries because of the flags of convenience that ensure that operating costs are cheaper than those of western Europe.

These flags do not always guarantee security, environmental protection or human rights, however. Sometimes certain flags of convenience hide distinctly unsavoury realities: ill-treated sailors, stowaways stripped and thrown overboard, oil slicks, traffic of arms and forbidden goods... (the two largest commercial fleets in the world are those of Liberia and Panama).

On some vessels you will find up to six different nationalities, represented by the country of construction, the flag, the nationality of the shipowner, the port of registry, the officers and finally the sailors!

New systems of navigation, communication and detection have led to crews being constantly reduced in size, even on the big ships. The consequence for passengers is that some boats are now built with a minimum number of cabins, and only the traditional shipowner's cabin or the pilot's cabin remain unoccupied... On other boats, on the other hand, the reduction in the number of crew has resulted in more cabins becoming available for passengers.

Passengers

The international organization which governs maritime safety is called IMO (International Maritime Organization) and has its headquarters in London. With regard to cargo ships, the rules state that it is obligatory to have a doctor on board if the ship is carrying more than 12 passengers—a totally arbitrary figure. This explains the maximum figure of 12 passengers which you will find in cargo ship voyages (except passenger-cargo ships).

So who exactly are these people who have chosen to travel on board cargo ships? The following response came from the passenger section at the Mediterranean Shipping Company in Geneva:

> Our clientele is made up of people who wish to travel differently, at a more civilized pace. Some are people who dislike travelling on aeroplanes, some are young adventure-seekers who want to explore the continent towards which they are heading port by port, and some are retired people for whom the voyage itself is an adventure.

You could no doubt add the following to the profile: ex-merchant navy sailors, hard-core sailors, artists in search of inspiration, writers looking for space out of time in order to write, musicians listening to another silence... not forgetting those who use cargo ship holds to transport furniture, import cars and motorbikes, or pets. Last but not least there are all those who have decided to take the time to live, and many more who can't be classified, who are nostalgic, dedicated to the sea and to boats.

English: The Language of Cargo Ships

English is the universal language of sailors and shipping companies, the symbol of economic prosperity derived from maritime transport. The language used on board ship, however, will depend on the nationality of the officers.

Luggage

Cargo ships offer fairly generous baggage allowances (often 150kg per person). Excess baggage is transported under the same conditions as the rest of the freight. (Polish Ocean Lines, for example, quote a figure of $1.50 per extra kilo.)

If you are taking heavy luggage and will require a porter, you should contact the port agents at least one day before departure.

Some vessels will accept cars, minibuses and two-wheeled vehicles.

Clothing

Whatever the latitude, you are likely to encounter fresh sea breezes at some point during your voyage, so make sure you have packed some warm clothing, and a waterproof or windcheater.

It is not advisable for women to wear shoes with heels.

Casual clothes are perfectly appropriate on cargo ships, but mealtimes are sometimes more formal, taken in the company of officers who are always in uniform. You should therefore take with you a few smarter items of clothing for this sort of occasion. There are even some old-fashioned cargo ships, like the *Argentina Star*, where men are requested to don jacket and tie for certain dinners.

Take along an alarm clock so you don't miss a sunrise, the first sight of land or even just breakfast!

Finally, don't forget to pack a pair of binoculars in your suitcase. They will be in constant use, scanning the horizon, observing other boats, sea mammals and of course receding or approaching land... Avoid high magnification lenses, which will blur your vision because of the boat's movements, and don't spend hours looking through your binoculars as it might make you sea-sick!

Sea-sickness

Some people never get it, others suffer chronically—including some sailors—and still others are afflicted occasionally. In most cases the sickness of the first day's sailing recedes during the crossing; the body gets used to the sea and adapts itself to the ship's movements.

The first signs of sea-sickness are weariness, yawning, sweating, feeling unwell. Anxiety makes things worse: fear of being sea-sick can bring it on!

One cause of sea-sickness can be an imbalance between the inner ear and vision. It is usually a good idea to go out on deck if you feel it coming on, keep active and look at the horizon. You should avoid confining yourself to your cabin, reading, or staring at the stem wave or the wake of the boat.

Sleeping is another way of overcoming sea-sickness. Traditional medicines are not recommended except for severe cases, as they can have harmful side effects. The Chinese apparently use a remedy based on ginger—you could always take a piece of root ginger on board in your pocket and nibble it from time to time!

And sometimes, as an old sailor friend told me, you just have to know how to vomit, simply and without stress, accepting that your body is doing you a favour and you will feel much better afterwards.

It's worth noting that cargo ships are more stable than liners, in that most of their hull is submerged, being loaded with freight. However, greater stability can lead to more violent lurches in heavy seas.

A liner, sitting higher in the water, offers more wind resistance; as its centre of gravity is situated higher it is more subject to rolling and pitching. Most passenger ships, however, are equipped with stabilizers which efficiently limit rolling.

Life on Board

A sea voyage is a voyage outside time. On land, people are always complaining that they don't have enough time. At sea these points of reference disappear. Social differences are easily forgotten: we are all human beings on a little vessel in the middle of an immense sea. A kind of rich fullness pervades us, contrasting with our attitude at port:

> It is interesting to note the change in one's attitude when we are in port versus when at sea. While in port there's the concern about going back to town 'one last time'—for whatever reason—since there may not be another opportunity. While at sea, there is no evidence of any indecision like this. There is something magical in the fact that we are going some

place. We don't care where or how fast, but we do care that we are not standing still. Life seems calm.

These words, written by Keith and Jean Comly on board the cargo ship *Columbia Star*, demonstrate the shift in attitude that occurs during a crossing.

It is astonishing how people on board ship find themselves a space, an activity: starting a diary, reading all those books they 'never had time to read', painting or drawing, listening to music, meditating, writing, watching a video, playing chess, cards, darts, chatting at the bar, playing music after dinner, singing...

Try to prepare for the long journey, therefore, by concentrating on your favourite activities, and take your 'spiritual food' with you.

For physical relaxation, you could dive into the small swimming pool on board, or else take advantage of the gym and sauna if the ship has them. You may also get the chance to play ping-pong, a game which takes on a whole new dimension when the ship rolls or pitches...

On board a cruise ship, passengers are entertained all day long, as if to try to make them forget that they are at sea and on a ship. On board a cargo ship the opposite is the case. Passengers and officers are in contact with each other and the progress of the vessel or the weather forecasts become natural subjects of conversation. If they are invited, passengers can also go up to the bridge or engine room. This allows them to become a part of the ship and follow its progress from day to day.

Casting off (departure) and docking (arrival) are events to be savoured. The entertaining manoeuvres of the tugs, pilots climbing like monkeys up rope ladders... How could one be bored with so much to see?

And, let's admit it, a cabin in a cargo ship on the ocean can also be a dream love nest for a couple looking for an unusual and timeless honeymoon. They say that sensuality is heightened on boats, that the high seas and pitching have 'a vertiginous effect on couples', as related by the Cuban writer Marya Montero in her erotic novel, *One Night With You*:

> *Bermudez, who is experienced in these matters—he hasn't been married three times for nothing—had warned me before the off: women really let themselves go on boats.*

Is it Possible to Hitchhike on Cargo Ships?

Is it still possible today, as it was in the old days, to go to a port and convince the captain of a cargo ship to take you on board, as either a paying passenger or a guest? In principle the answer is no and the same reasons are always quoted:

insurance problems, no doctor or steward on board, the need for company authorization, etc. However, there are exceptions.

This was the case with Andreas, a German traveller who had disembarked from a sailing boat in the Azores. Seeking to return to Europe by sea, he went round all the cargo ships in port, to be met with refusal after refusal, until the day when he encountered the captain of a Greek company who accepted him on board his cargo ship bound for Portugal. During the crossing the two men became firm friends, so much so that on their arrival the captain announced that Andreas would be a permanent guest on any of the company's other boats as well.

Another example is that of Manu and Rachel, from St Pierre-et-Miquelon, who, having covered a good number of miles on their sailing boat, arrived in France on board a small cargo ship. Manu recalls:

> The Ville de Corte, a ro-ro of 80m, was more accustomed to crossing the Mediterranean between North Africa and Marseilles than facing the cold and ice. For 5 months it operated a round trip from Halifax to St-Pierre to Miquelon every 10 days. It replaced our usual ro-ro which was being completely refurbished.
>
> Since we knew the shipowner and the captain, we had no difficulty embarking on the return voyage to Marseilles. Our cabin was situated in a container behind the wheelhouse... Four containers were laid out in this way to accommodate the lorry drivers who were crossing the Mediterranean.

It was an unusual 10-day crossing which began in the ice fields of Saint-Laurent, under a magical light, and finished in the smog of Marseilles...

There are always exceptions, of course, but a perusal of the books of Gavin Young, who has sailed the oceans of the world in dozens of boats, shows us that with determination and resourcefulness all obstacles can be overcome in order to travel by ship.

Never forget that a captain has the power to invite anyone on board; some officers invite their partners for the length of the voyage.

How to Work Out the Price of a Ticket Between Two Ports of Call

An arrival point for one person may be a point of departure for another, which is why the voyages detailed in this guide can be read from any port of call.

In most cases the ticket price refers to a round trip. If you know the length of the voyage you can calculate the daily fare and the price between two ports of call.

For instance, look at the following itinerary:

Itinerary

Round trip: about 16 days

▼

Hamburg *Germany*	Jeddah *Saudi Arabia*
Antwerp *Belgium*	Suez Canal
Le Havre *France*	Gibraltar
Gibraltar	Le Havre *France*
Piraeus *Greece*	Hamburg *Germany*
Suez Canal	

Fare for the round trip: US$1600, or US$100 per day.

The round trip includes Hamburg to Hamburg, via Jeddah. You may just be interested in the Le Havre–Piraeus section. How would you work out the price of the ticket?

You need to find out either the number of days spent at sea, or the distance between the two ports. In this case, Le Havre to Piraeus is 2693 miles. Basing our figures on the fact that most cargo ships sail at between 15 and 20 knots per hour, we can calculate the time the ship will take. The journey from Le Havre to Piraeus works out at about 7 days, without counting the ports of call. At $100 a day, you can therefore estimate the ticket price to be around $700, to which of course you should add the equivalent price for the ports of call and any port taxes.

Reed's Marine Distance Tables is a useful little book, the stuff of seafarers' dreams, packed with numbers and listing the distances between all the major ports of the world (more than 500 ports are listed in the index). It allows shipowners and ship brokers to calculate the most direct routes for their boats. It is published in the UK by Thomas Reed, 19 Bridge Road, Hampton Court, East Molesey, Surrey KT8 9EU, ✆ (0181) 941 7878.

In order to allow you to transcribe nautical miles into days spent travelling, here is the time a cargo ship sailing at 15 knots takes to cover certain distances:

> For 500 miles: 1 day and 9 hours
>
> For 1000 miles: 2 days and 19 hours
>
> For 2000 miles: 5 days and 13 hours
>
> For 3000 miles: 8 days and 8 hours
>
> For 5000 miles: 13 days and 21 hours
>
> For 10,000 miles: 27 days and 18 hours
>
> (Excluding ports of call)

One nautical mile = 1852 metres.
One knot = unit of speed equivalent to one marine mile per hour.

Below are the distances from Felixstowe and Los Angeles to several major ports around the world. This will help you make a few estimates.

Distances in Nautical Miles from Felixstowe to Ports around the World

Alexandria	3107	Jakarta	8515
Antwerp	193	Jeddah	3960
Aqaba	3639	Karachi	6090
Auckland	11,290	Kingston	4250
Baltimore	3500	Lagos	4240
Bangkok	9290	Los Angeles	7677
Barcelona	1834	Marseilles	1996
Bombay	6296	Mauritius	6955
Brisbane	12,060	Mombasa	6255
Buenos Aires	6330	Montreal	3135
Calcutta	7955	New Orleans	4810
Callao	6107	New York	3200
Cape Town	6150	Osaka	10,940
Cartagena	4510	Papeete (via Panama Canal)	9300
Casablanca	1363	Philadelphia	3350
Dar es Salaam	6355	Piraeus	2815
Galveston	5000	Port Said	3236
Genoa	2164	Recife	4115
Gibraltar	1301	Rio de Janeiro	5200
Guayaquil	5612	Seattle	8804
Halifax	2635	Singapore	8280
Le Havre	205	Suez	3335
Ho Chi Minh City	8905	Sydney (via Suez)	11,590
Hong Kong	9715	Tokyo	11,253
Honolulu (via Panama Canal)	9470	Valparaiso	7378
Izmir	2930	Vancouver	8847

Distances in Nautical Miles from Los Angeles to Ports around the World

Alexandria	9090	Karachi	10,749
Antwerp	7753	Kingston	3507
Aqaba (via Panama Canal)	9596	Lagos (via Panama Canal)	8006
Auckland	5658	London	7677
Baltimore	4857	Mauritius	10,471
Bangkok	7948	Mombasa (via Panama Canal)	11,908
Bombay	10,308	Montreal	6210
Buenos Aires (via Magellan)	7243	New Orleans	4346
Calcutta	9505	New York	4930
Callao	3654	Osaka	5193
Cape Town (via Panama Canal)	9421	Papeete	3571
Cartagena	3237	Philadelphia	4902
Casablanca	7150	Piraeus	8790
Dar es Salaam	11,399	Port Said	9210
Galveston	4449	Recife (via Panama Canal)	6173
Genoa	8145	Rio de Janeiro (via Panama)	7245
Guayaquil	3228	Seattle	1128
Halifax	5251	Singapore	7867
Le Havre	7557	Suez (via Panama Canal)	9296
Ho Chi Minh City	7291	Sydney	6511
Hong Kong	6380	Tokyo	4857
Honolulu	2231	Valparaiso	4806
Jakarta	7356	Vancouver	1144
Jeddah (via Panama Canal)	9933	Veracruz	4376

Index of Ports

At the back of the book you will find an index of all the ports mentioned in this guide. This will enable you to locate all the passenger cargo ships which stop there.

How to Use This Guide

Preliminary Remarks

We have endeavoured to make this guidebook as complete as possible, and it is, to our knowledge, the first of its kind. We have had to invent certain classifications in order to enable the traveller to locate the numerous itineraries of cargo ships which criss-cross the world in all directions. When dealing with a subject as variable as the merchant navy, one quickly comes across numerous difficulties in establishing a conventional and infallible guidebook.

Absolute precision is impossible when it comes to sailing. Itineraries follow a logic that is more commercial than geographical (and that's when the weather doesn't intervene). Shipping companies always take the precaution of emphasizing to passengers that everything—or almost everything—is subject to change.

However, new means of communication and navigation have improved the reliability of timetables and itineraries to such an extent that these days some container ship voyages can be as punctual as a train journey—which is in direct contrast to the unpredictable wanderings of the tramp steamers.

Choosing Your Destination

In the first part of this guide, each section deals with a specific destination:

1.   USA and Canada
2.   Mexico, the Caribbean, Central America and South America
3.   The Mediterranean, Africa, the south Atlantic islands, the Red Sea, the Near and Middle East, the Indian Ocean islands
4.   India, Southeast Asia, the Far East, Australia, New Zealand, New Caledonia, the Pacific
5.   Scandinavia, Iceland, the Baltic, Russia
6.   Round-the-world lines
7.   Voyages outside Europe.

For convenience, the destinations in each section are listed from north to south. Thus, a voyage from Europe to Montreal will precede a voyage to New York, which itself precedes a voyage to New Orleans, etc.

Itineraries are set out in the chronological order of the ports of call (the countries or regions are indicated in *italics*). After the itinerary you will find the name of the company or agency which supplies the ticket, plus the page to turn to.

For the traveller, a port of call can be either a point of departure or a point of arrival. The first port mentioned need not be your port of departure. Thus, in the case of the following itinerary: 'Hamburg–Antwerp–Le Havre–Montreal–New York–Le Havre–Antwerp–Hamburg', you could choose to embark at Le Havre and disembark at

Montreal, but you could also embark at Montreal to get back to Le Havre or Antwerp, in the knowledge that the boat will travel via New York, and so on...

In some cases the country alone is indicated and you should contact the company or relevant agency to find out the name of the port at the time of your departure. When two ports are indicated as follows: 'Rotterdam/Antwerp', the vessel will make a port of call at either Rotterdam or Antwerp, depending on its freight. Similarly, the itinerary for some voyages will list a series of ports in western Europe (Hamburg, Bremen, Rotterdam, Felixstowe, Antwerp, Le Havre), for example; however, this does not necessarily mean that the ship will call at each port.

You will not always find the cargo ship of your dreams leaving from a port near you. The major ports of Europe are Felixstowe, Tilbury and Thamesport (UK), Le Havre (France), Antwerp (Belgium), Rotterdam (Holland), Bremen and Hamburg (Germany), Genoa and Livorno (Italy) and Valencia (Spain).

Thanks to the port index, you can use the guide wherever you are in the world. When selecting a cargo ship you are choosing not only a destination but a whole itinerary.

Some voyages will appear twice in the list of itineraries if they cover two distinct areas of the world during the same trip. Thus a 'Europe–Senegal–Brazil–Europe' tour will be included in both the African and South American sections.

Choosing a Shipping Company

The second section of the guide contains an alphabetical list of shipping companies corresponding to your chosen voyage. All conditions relating to the voyage are listed. Look at the daily fares to compare the prices of two companies.

Round-the-world Lines

The development of container ships has allowed some companies to put regular round-the-world lines into service (usually heading in a westerly direction, i.e. from Europe to Panama and the Pacific); these round trips operate 365 days of the year.

The voyages take from 80 to 100 days, with numerous ports of call on several continents, and are mostly sold as round trips—a round-the-world voyage returning you to your port of embarkation. Although it is not always easy to find accommodation on board between ports of call, as these trips are very popular, particularly amongst retired people, there is nothing to stop you contacting the relevant companies to find out whether there is a spare cabin between any two ports of call which may interest you (between Europe and the South Pacific, for example).

Catching a Tramp Steamer en Route

It is important to note that tramp steamers do not have fixed advance itineraries; their routes and ports of call are dictated by supply and demand. They are liable to be sent anywhere in the world. You should therefore contact companies such as Egon Oldendorff, Mineral Shipping, Dobson Lines and others to find out the positions of their vessels and their planned routes during the weeks to come.

If you are not set on a particular destination, why not just leave on a whim? Tramp steamers offer inexpensive last-minute voyages to more or less anywhere.

Trial Runs

For those who wish to do a trial run before setting off on a long voyage, this guidebook offers various short trips—to the Baltic, the North Sea, the Atlantic and the Mediterranean. Short journeys may not conjure up the timeless atmosphere of long crossings, but they will give you a taste of life on board a cargo ship, and timetables for short journeys are more reliable.

Treasure Hunt

There are many ways of finding a suitable vessel for travelling. This book offers as many options as possible, but cargo ship voyages are affected by all sorts of variable circumstances and you will discover other routes and other ships by using the information in this book as a starting point.

Finding a cargo ship on which to travel can be the simplest thing in the world, as there are regular lines with several departures per month as well as specialist agencies who can help. On the other hand, you may be flicking lazily through this guide and come across the voyage of your dreams or a departing tramp steamer... You can also do your own research and find new solutions and unexpected itineraries.

Warning

For practical information, we depend on the shipping companies and agencies who supplied us with details. This information is constantly changing.

With regard to cargo ships, fares are, like the itineraries, subject to change at all times.

Prices

The prices are given in US dollars (US$), deutschmarks (DM), pounds sterling (£), French francs (F), or others, depending on the country of issue.

The first price given is the lowest price, the second the highest.

Telephone Numbers

The international dialling codes are given after each telephone number.

Itineraries

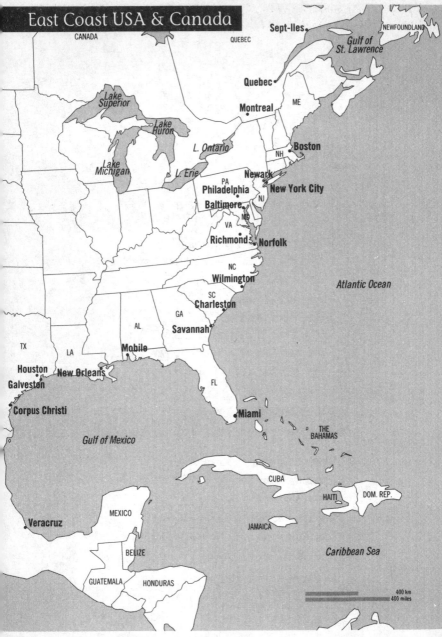

East Coast USA & Canada

CANADA

QUEBEC

NEWFOUNDLAND

Sept-Iles

Gulf of
St. Lawrence

Quebec

Montreal

ME

Lake
Superior

Lake
Huron

L. Ontario

NH

Boston

Lake
Michigan

L. Erie

Newark

PA

Philadelphia

New York City

NJ

Baltimore

MD

VA

Richmond

Norfolk

NC

Wilmington

Atlantic Ocean

SC

Charleston

GA

Savannah

AL

Mobile

TX

LA

Houston

New Orleans

Galveston

FL

Corpus Christi

Miami

THE
BAHAMAS

Gulf of Mexico

CUBA

MEXICO

HAITI

DOM. REP.

Veracruz

JAMAICA

BELIZE

Caribbean Sea

GUATEMALA

HONDURAS

400 km
400 miles

46

▶ Europe

&

▶ USA

▶ Canada

1   Egon Oldendorff, p.136

▼ A western European port

   often:
   Ghent *Belgium*
   Rotterdam *Holland*
   Le Havre *France*
   Hamburg *Germany*

   Sept-Iles/Port-Cartier/
   Baie-Comeau *Canada*

Montreal/Quebec *Canada*

occasionally:
ports on the Great Lakes

Quebec *Canada*

A western European port

2   Mediterranean Great Lakes Line, p.159

▼ Montreal *Canada*
   Liverpool *United Kingdom*
   Le Havre *France*
   Montreal *Canada*
   or:
   Montreal *Canada*

Mediterranean ports such as:

Koper *Slovenia*
Trieste *Italy*
Naples/Salerno *Italy*
Genoa *Italy*
Spain
occasionally: Portugal

Montreal *Canada*

3   Containerschiffs Reederei, p.130

▼ Genoa *Italy*   Montreal *Canada*
Valencia *Spain*   Salerno *Italy*
Cadiz *Spain*   Livorno *Italy*
Lisbon *Portugal*   Genoa *Italy*

4   N.S.B., p.169

▼ Salerno *Italy*   Cadiz *Spain*
Livorno *Italy*   Lisbon *Portugal*
Genoa *Italy*   Montreal *Canada*
Valencia *Spain*   Salerno *Italy*

5   Deutsche Seereederei Rostock, PZ, p.131

▼ Livorno/Genoa *Italy*   Izmir *Turkey*
Valencia *Spain*   Naples *Italy*
Montreal *Canada*   Genoa/Livorno *Italy*
Larnaka *Cyprus*

6   Mediterranean Shipping Company, p.160

▼ Antwerp *Belgium*   Boston *Massachusetts USA*
Hamburg *Germany*   New York *USA*
Bremen *Germany*   Baltimore *Maryland USA*
Felixstowe *United Kingdom*   Norfolk *Virginia USA*
Le Havre *France*   Antwerp *Belgium*

7 — Egon Oldendorff, p.137

▼ Antwerp *Belgium*
Rotterdam *Holland*
Bremen *Germany*
Felixstowe *United Kingdom*
Wilmington *North Carolina USA*
Charleston *South Carolina USA*
Miami *Florida USA*
New Orleans *Louisiana USA*

Houston *Texas USA*
Charleston *South Carolina USA*
Wilmington *North Carolina USA*
Antwerp *Belgium*
Bremen *Germany*
Felixstowe *United Kingdom*
Le Havre *France*

8 — Mineral Shipping, p.167

▼ Savannah *Georgia USA*
Rotterdam/Delfzijl *Holland*
Searsport *Massachusetts USA*
Wilmington *North Carolina USA*

or:
Georgetown *South Carolina USA*
Savannah *Georgia USA*

9 — Independent, agent: Strand Cruise & Travel, p.203

▼ Antwerp *Belgium*
Chester *Pennsylvania USA*
Richmond *Virginia USA*

possibly:
Chester *Pennsylvania USA*
Antwerp *Belgium*

10 — Egon Oldendorff, p.137

▼ A western European port
  often:
  Ghent *Belgium*
  Rotterdam *Holland*
  Le Havre *France*
  Hamburg *Germany*

Norfolk/Newport News
  Virginia USA

occasionally:
Baltimore *Maryland USA*
Philadelphia *Pennsylvania USA*
Newark *New York USA*
Boston *Massachusetts USA*

A western European port

11   Mediterranean Shipping Company, p.161

▼ Antwerp *Belgium*
   Rotterdam *Holland*
   Felixstowe *United Kingdom*
   Wilmington *North Carolina USA*
   Charleston *South Carolina USA*
   Miami *Florida USA*

New Orleans *Louisiana USA*
Houston *Texas USA*
Charleston *South Carolina USA*
Wilmington *North Carolina USA*
Antwerp *Belgium*

12   Egon Oldendorff, p.138

▼ A western European port
   often:
   Ghent *Belgium*
   Rotterdam *Holland*
   Le Havre *France*
   Hamburg *Germany*

Ports in southeastern USA:
   New Orleans *Louisiana*
   Mobile *Alabama*
   Houston *Texas*
   Galveston *Texas*
   Corpus Christi *Texas*
A western European port

13   Agent: Frachtschiff-Touristik, p.203

▼ La Spezia *Italy*
   Barcelona *Spain*
   Valencia *Spain*
   Miami *Florida USA*

Houston *Texas USA*
New Orleans *Louisiana USA*
La Spezia *Italy*

14   N.S.B., p.169

▼ La Spezia *Italy*
   Miami *Florida USA*
   Houston *Texas USA*
   New Orleans *Louisiana USA*

Valencia *Spain*
Barcelona *Spain*
La Spezia *Italy*

▼ A port in southeastern USA

A Mediterranean port

   possibly in:

   Morocco

   Italy

Tunisia

Egypt

Israel

Turkey

Galveston *Texas USA*

Central & South America

USA

Puerto Rico (U.S.)   **San Juan**   British Virgin Islands (U.K.)

Ponce   Virgin Islands (U.S.)   North Antilles (NETH.)   ANTIGUA AND BARBUDA

Pointe-à-Pitre

GUADELOUPE

DOMINICA

Fort-de-France   MARTINIQUE

ST. LUCIA

BARBADOS   **Bridgetown**

ST. VINCENT AND THE GRENADINES

GRENADA

Straits of Florida

THE BAHAMAS

Tampico

Veracruz

Yucatan Channel

CUBA

Cayman Islands (U.K.)

JAMAICA

HAITI   DOM. REP.   Puerto Rico (U.S.)

Kingston   **Port-au-Prince**

MEXICO   BELIZE   **Puerto Cortés**

Caribbean Sea

Aruba   **Willemstad**

Port of Spain

TRINIDAD AND TOBAGO

Port-of-Spain

GUATEMALA   HONDURAS

EL SALVADOR   NICARAGUA

Corinto   **Puerto Limon**

COSTA RICA   PANAMA

Panama

La Guaira

Caracas

Cartagena

VENEZUELA

Georgetown

GUYANA   **Paramaribo**

SURINAME   **Cayenne**

FRENCH GUIANA (FRANCE)

North Atlantic Ocean

Bogota

Buenaventura

COLOMBIA

San Lorenzo

Quito

ECUADOR   **Guayaquil**

Galapagos Islands (ECU.)

PERU

Manaus

Santarém

Belém

Fortaleza

BRAZIL

Trujillo

Natal

Recife

Callao   **Lima**

Salvador

La Paz

BOLIVIA

Brasilia

Arica

Iquique

CHILE

PARAGUAY

Asunción

Vitória

Rio de Janeiro

Antofagasta

Paranaguá   **Santos**

Itajai

Porto Alegre

Valparaiso   **Santiago**

URUGUAY   **Rio Grande**

San Antonio

Buenos Aires   **Montevideo**

Talcahuano

ARGENTINA

Mar del Plata

South Pacific Ocean

South Atlantic Ocean

Puerto Montt

FALKLAND ISLANDS (U.K.)

500 km

500 miles

Punta Arenas   **Ushuaia**

SOUTH GEORGIA ISLAND (U.K.)

52

▶ Europe

&

▶ Mexico

▶ The Caribbean

▶ Central America

▶ South America

▶ Mexico, the Caribbean, Central America

16	Agent: Strand Cruise & Travel, p.203

▼ Amsterdam *Holland*   Antwerp *Belgium*
Cuba   Amsterdam *Holland*
possibly: Mexico

17	Agent: Hamburger Abendblatt/Die Welt, p.220

▼ Hamburg *Germany*   Quetzal *Guatemala*
Bremen *Germany*   Corinto *Nicaragua*
Antwerp *Belgium*   Buenaventura *Colombia*
Rio Haina *Dominican Republic*   San Lorenzo *Ecuador*
Cartagena *Colombia*   Panama Canal
Panama Canal   Bremen *Germany*
Caldera *Costa Rica*   Hamburg *Germany*
Acajutla *San Salvador*

18   Deutsche Seereederei Rostock, p.132

▼ Hamburg *Germany*
San Juan *Puerto Rico*
Veracruz *Mexico*
Tampico *Mexico*
possibly: La Guaira *Venezuela*

Rio Haina *Dominican Republic*
San Juan *Puerto Rico*
Antwerp *Belgium*
Hamburg *Germany*

19   Egon Oldendorff, p.137

▼ Antwerp *Belgium*
Bremen *Germany*
Felixstowe *United Kingdom*
Le Havre *France*
Boston *Massachusetts USA*
Charleston *South Carolina USA*
Miami *Florida USA*
Veracruz *Mexico*
Altamira *Mexico*

Galveston *Texas USA*
Houston *Texas USA*
New Orleans *Louisiana USA*
Charleston *South Carolina USA*
Boston *Massachusetts USA*
Antwerp *Belgium*
Bremen *Germany*
Felixstowe *United Kingdom*
Le Havre *France*

20   Lykes Line, p.155

▼ Felixstowe *United Kingdom*
Antwerp *Belgium*
Bremen *Germany*

Le Havre *France*
New Orleans *Louisiana USA*
Galveston *Texas USA*

21   C.G.M., p.123

▼ Le Havre *France*
Fort-de-France *Martinique*

or Pointe-à-Pitre *Guadeloupe*
Le Havre *France*

▼ Hamburg *Germany*
Le Havre *France*
Pointe-à-Pitre *Guadeloupe*
Fort-de-France *Martinique*
St Lucia (*occasional calls*)

Moin *Costa Rica*
Dover *United Kingdom*
Antwerp *Belgium*
Hamburg *Germany*

▼ Antwerp/Ghent *Belgium*
Puerto Cabello *Venezuela*

La Guaira/Maracaïbo
Venezuela

▼ A western European port
La Guaira *Venezuela*
Cartagena *Colombia*
Panama
Puerto Limon *Costa Rica*

Santo Tomas de Castilla
Guatemala
Veracruz *Mexico*
New Orleans/Houston *USA*
A western European port

▼ Bremen *Germany*
Rotterdam *Holland*
Felixstowe *United Kingdom*
Paramaribo *Surinam*
Georgetown *Guyana*
Port of Spain *Trinidad*
La Guaira *Venezuela*

Willemstad *Curaçao*
Oranjestad *Aruba*
Cartagena *Colombia*
Puerto Cabello *Venezuela*
Guanta *Venezuela*
Rotterdam *Holland*
Bremen *Germany*

▶ East Coast of South America

26 Hartman, agent: Hamburger Abendblatt/Die Welt, p.221

▼ Sète *France*
  or Valencia *Spain*
  Marina di Carrara *Italy*
  Marseilles *France*
  Banjul *Gambia*

Degrad des Cannes
  French Guyana
Belem *Brazil*
Valencia *Spain*
  or Sète *France*

27 Parten, agent: Strand Cruise & Travel, p.204

▼ Antwerp *Belgium*
  Santanas (Amazon) *Brazil*
  Manaus (Amazon) *Brazil*
  Itacoatiara (Amazon) *Brazil*

Belem *Brazil*
Rouen/Honfleur *France*
Bremen *Germany*

28 Dollart Reederei, p.134

▼ Genoa *Italy*
  Fos-sur-mer *France*
  Barcelona *Spain*
  Fortaleza *Brazil*
  Salvador *Brazil*
  Santos *Brazil*
  Buenos Aires *Argentina*
  Montevideo *Uruguay*
  Sao Francisco do Sul *Brazil*

Vitoria *Brazil*
Salvador *Brazil*
Tenerife *Canary Islands*
Las Palmas *Canary Islands*
Valencia *Spain*
Livorno *Italy*
Naples *Italy*
Genoa *Italy*

29 — Blue Star Line, p.119

▼ Tilbury *United Kingdom*
Hamburg *Germany*
Bremen *Germany*
Antwerp *Belgium*
Recife/Suape *Brazil*
Santos *Brazil*
Rio Grande *Brazil*
Itajai *Brazil*
Santos *Brazil*
Rio de Janeiro *Brazil*
Salvador *Brazil*
Le Havre *France*
Rotterdam *Holland*
Tilbury *United Kingdom*
Itinerary may vary to include other ports: Buenos Aires *Argentina* and Lisbon *Portugal*

30 — Peter Dohle, p.182

▼ Tilbury *United Kingdom*
Hamburg *Germany*
Bremen *Germany*
Rotterdam *Holland*
Antwerp *Belgium*
Le Havre *France*
Bilbao *Spain*
Santos *Brazil*
Buenos Aires *Argentina*
Montevideo *Uruguay*
Sao Francisco do Sul *Brazil*
Tilbury *United Kingdom*

31 — Grimaldi, p.142

▼ Tilbury *United Kingdom*
Hamburg *Germany*
Emden *Germany*
Rotterdam *Holland*
Antwerp *Belgium*
Le Havre *France*
Vitoria *Brazil*
Santos *Brazil*
Paranagua *Brazil*
Rio de Janeiro *Brazil*
Tilbury *United Kingdom*

32   Polish Ocean Lines, p.184

▼ Gdynia *Poland*
  A western European port
  Buenos Aires *Argentina*
  Montevideo *Uruguay*

Santos *Brazil*
Rio de Janeiro *Brazil*
Salvador *Brazil*
A western European port

33   Mineral Shipping, p.167

▼ Genoa *Italy*
  Livorno *Italy*
  Ancona *Italy*
  Monfalcone *Italy*
  Porto Vesme *Sardinia*

Yeraniki *Greece*
Munguba (Amazon) *Brazil*
Rotterdam *Holland*
Hamburg *Germany*
Bremen *Germany*

34   Grimaldi Lines, p.142

▼ Genoa *Italy*
  Paranagua *Brazil*
  Santos *Brazil*
  Rio de Janeiro *Brazil*

Salerno *Italy*
Livorno *Italy*
Genoa *Italy*

35   Jugolinija, p.151

▼ Rijeka *Croatia*
  (*different destinations depending on voyage*)

Buenos Aires *Argentina*
Rijeka *Croatia*

▶ West Coast of South America

36   Polish Ocean Lines, p.185

▼ Gdynia *Poland*
   A western European port
   Panama Canal
   Guayaquil *Ecuador*
   Callao *Peru*
   Arica *Chile*

Antofagasta *Chile*
Valparaiso *Chile*
Straits of Magellan
Brazil
A western European port
Gdynia *Poland*

37   Reederei Oltmann, agent: Strand Cruise & Travel, p.204

▼ Hamburg *Germany*
   Antwerp *Belgium*
   Bilbao *Spain*
   Panama Canal
   Iquique *Chile*
   Valparaiso *Chile*
   Talcahuano *Chile*
   San Antonio *Chile*

Antofagasta *Chile*
Arica *Chile*
Guayaquil *Ecuador*
Panama Canal
Bilbao *Spain*
Antwerp *Belgium*
Hamburg *Germany*

38   Mediterranean Shipping Company, p.161

▼ Antwerp *Belguim*
   Rotterdam *Holland*
   Bremerhaven *Germany*
   Hamburg *Germany*
   Felixstowe *United Kingdom*
   Charleston *South Carolina USA*
   (change vessels)
   Panama Canal

Guayaquil *Ecuador*
Callao *Peru*
Valparaiso *Chile*
Arica *Chile*
Callao *Peru*
Guayaquil *Ecuador*
Charleston *South Carolina USA*

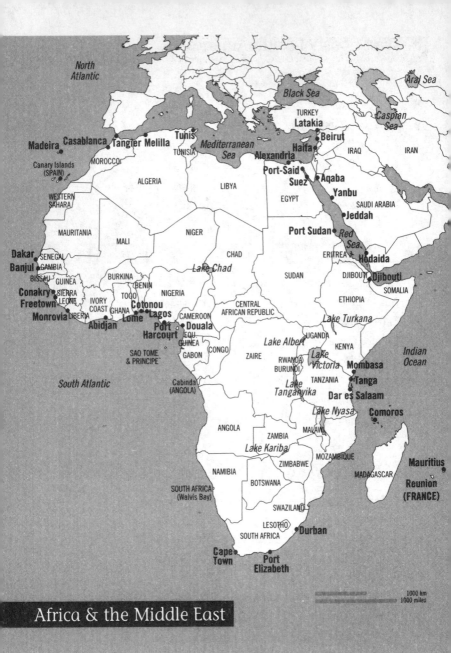

Africa & the Middle East

Voyages between ▶

> ▶ Europe
>
> &
>
> ▶ Mediterranean
> ▶ Africa
> ▶ Islands in the Atlantic Ocean
> ▶ The Red Sea
> ▶ Near and Middle East
> ▶ Islands in the Indian Ocean

▶ The Mediterranean and Middle East

39   O.P.D.R., agent: Strand Cruise & Travel, p.205

▼ Hamburg *Germany*
Felixstowe *United Kingdom*
Rotterdam *Holland*
Gibraltar
Ceuta (*Spanish territory in Morocco*)

Melilla (*Spanish territory in Morocco*)
Cartagena *Spain*
Cadiz *Spain*
Rotterdam *Holland*
Hamburg *Germany*

40   Projex Line, p.187

▼ Felixstowe *United Kingdom*
Hamburg/Bremen *Germany*
Rotterdam *Holland*
Antwerp *Belgium*
Tunis *Tunisia*
Alexandria *Egypt*
Port Said *Egypt*

Beirut *Lebanon*
Mersin *Turkey*
Istanbul *Turkey*
Salonika *Greece*
Izmir *Turkey*
Salerno *Italy*
Felixstowe *United Kingdom*

41   Reederei Dede, agent: Strand Cruise & Travel, p.205

▼ Rotterdam *Holland*
Antwerp *Belgium*
Piraeus *Greece*
Salonika *Greece*

Istanbul *Turkey*
Izmir *Turkey*
Rotterdam *Holland*

42   Grimaldi, p.143

▼ Gothenburg *Sweden*
Antwerp *Belgium*
Southampton *United Kingdom*
Livorno *Italy*
Piraeus *Greece*

Limassol *Cyprus*
Ashdod *Israel*
Salerno/Savona *Italy*
A western European port

43   Agent: Hamburger Abendblatt/Die Welt, p.222

▼ Rotterdam *Holland*
Tilbury *United Kingdom*
Piraeus *Greece*
Izmir *Turkey*

Piraeus *Greece*
Felixstowe *United Kingdom*
Rotterdam *Holland*

44   Containerschiffs Reederei, p.130

▼ Rotterdam *Holland*
Algeciras *Spain*
Piraeus *Greece*
Izmir *Turkey*
Salonika *Greece*

Piraeus *Greece*
Algeciras *Spain*
Felixstowe *United Kingdom*
Rotterdam *Holland*

▼ Felixstowe *United Kingdom*
Algeciras *Spain*
Piraeus *Greece*
Izmir *Turkey*
Salonika *Greece*

Piraeus *Greece*
Algeciras *Spain*
Rotterdam *Holland*
Felixstowe *United Kingdom*

▼ Hamburg *Germany*
Rotterdam *Holland*
Valletta *Malta*
Piraeus *Greece*
Heraklion *Crete*
Limassol *Cyprus*
Mersin *Turkey*

Salonika *Greece*
Istanbul *Turkey*
Burgas (*Black Sea, Bulgaria*)
Izmir *Turkey*
Le Havre *France*
Felixstowe *United Kingdom*
Hamburg *Germany*

▼ Rotterdam *Holland*
Gibraltar
Piraeus *Greece*
Limassol *Cyprus*
Alexandria *Egypt*
Ashdod *Israel*
Haifa *Israel*

Tartus *Syria*
Izmir *Turkey*
Salerno *Italy*
Gibraltar
Tilbury *United Kingdom*
Antwerp *Belgium*
Rotterdam *Holland*

48 — Interorient, agent: Hamburg-Süd, p.219

▼ Hamburg *Germany*
Bremen *Germany*
Rotterdam *Holland*
Limassol *Cyprus*

Ashdod *Israel*
Haifa *Israel*
Bremen *Germany*
Hamburg *Germany*

49 — Polish Ocean Lines, p.185

▼ Gdynia *Poland*
A western European port
Casablanca *Morocco*
Valletta *Malta*
Tunis *Tunisia*

Alexandria *Egypt*
Lattakia *Syria*
Limassol *Cyprus*
A western European port
Gdynia *Poland*

50 — Agent: Hamburger Abendblatt/Die Welt, p.222

▼ Hamburg/Bremen *Germany*
Rotterdam *Holland*
Antwerp *Belgium*
Alexandria *Egypt*
Port Said *Egypt*
Beirut *Lebanon*

Tartus *Syria*
Lattakia *Syria*
Mersin/Izmir *Turkey*
Salerno *Italy*
Felixstowe *United Kingdom*
Hamburg/Bremen *Germany*

51 — Agent: Hamburg-Süd, p.219

▼ Hamburg *Germany*
Rotterdam *Holland*
Antwerp *Belgium*
Malta
Alexandria *Egypt*
Beirut *Lebanon*

Tartus *Syria*
Lattakia *Syria*
Mersin/Izmir *Turkey*
Salerno *Italy*
Felixstowe *United Kingdom*
Hamburg *Germany*

▼ Hamburg *Germany*
Rotterdam *Holland*
Antwerp *Belgium*
Tunis *Tunisia*
Alexandria *Egypt*
Beirut *Lebanon*
Tartus *Syria*

Istanbul *Turkey*
Salonika *Greece*
Izmir *Turkey*
Salerno *Italy*
Felixstowe *United Kingdom*
Hamburg *Germany*

▼ Antwerp *Belgium*
Felixstowe *United Kingdom*
Alexandria *Egypt*
Ashdod *Israel*
Haifa *Israel*
Limassol *Cyprus*

every other week:
Naples *Italy*
every other week:
Livorno *Italy*
Antwerp *Belgium*

54   Agent: Hamburger-Abendblatt/Die Welt, p.222

▼ Rotterdam *Holland*   Le Havre *France*
   Santurce/Bilbao *Spain*   Rotterdam *Holland*

55   Reederei Russ, agent: Strand Cruise & Travel, p.206

▼ A western European port   Boulogne *France*
   Santander/Bilbao *Spain*   Blyth *United Kingdom*
   Antwerp *Belgium*   Dundee *United Kingdom*

56   Agent: Hamburger Abendblatt/Die Welt, p.223

▼ Rotterdam *Holland*   Leixoes *Portugal*
   Lisbon *Portugal*   Lisbon *Portugal*
   Leixoes *Portugal*   Vigo *Spain*
   Vigo *Spain*   Le Havre *France*
   Le Havre *France*   Rotterdam *Holland*
   Antwerp *Belgium*

57   Ramstad Shipping, agent: Strand Cruise & Travel, p.206

▼ Rotterdam *Holland*   Leixoes *Portugal*
   Lisbon *Portugal*   Rotterdam *Holland*

▼ Rotterdam *Holland*
  Antwerp *Belgium*
  Tangier *Morocco*
  Gibraltar
  Cadiz *Spain*

  Casablanca *Morocco*
  Cadiz *Spain*
  Felixstowe *United Kingdom*
  Rotterdam *Holland*

▼ Rotterdam *Holland*
  Antwerp *Belgium*
  Tangier *Morocco*

  Casablanca *Morocco*
  Rotterdam *Holland*

▼ A western European port
  (Bremen/Rotterdam/Antwerp)
  Casablanca *Morocco*

  A western European port
  (Bremen/Rotterdam/Antwerp)

▼ Bremen *Germany*
  Antwerp *Belgium*
  Casablanca *Morocco*
  Bremen *Germany*/
    Rotterdam *Holland*

  Antwerp *Belgium*
  Tangier *Morocco*
  Casablanca *Morocco*
  Rotterdam *Holland*

▼ Hamburg *Germany*
  Felixstowe *United Kingdom*
  Rotterdam *Holland*
  Funchal *Madeira*
  Las Palmas *Canary Islands*

Santa Cruz de Tenerife
  Canary Islands
possibly:
Casablanca *Morocco*
Cadiz *Spain*
Hamburg *Germany*

▼ Tilbury *United Kingdom*
  Hamburg *Germany*
  Amsterdam *Holland*
  Antwerp *Belgium*
  Le Havre *France*
  Dakar *Senegal*
  Conakry *Guinea*

Freetown *Sierra Leone*
Cotonou *Benin*
Lomé *Togo*
Tema *Ghana*
Lagos *Nigeria*
Douala *Cameroon*
Tilbury *United Kingdom*

▼ Hamburg *Germany*
  Antwerp *Belgium*
  Rotterdam *Holland*
  Felixstowe *United Kingdom*
  Le Havre *France*
  Dakar *Senegal*
  Conakry *Guinea*
  Freetown *Sierra Leone*
  Abidjan *Ivory Coast*
  Tema *Ghana*
  Lomé *Togo*

Cotonou *Benin*
Lagos *Nigeria*
Libreville *Gabon*
Douala *Cameroon*
Abidjan *Ivory Coast*
Dakar *Senegal*
Leixoes *Portugal*
Antwerp *Belgium*
Hamburg *Germany*
Tilbury *United Kingdom*

▼ Hamburg *Germany*
Rotterdam *Holland*
Antwerp *Belgium*
Le Havre *France*
possibly:
Las Palmas *Canary Islands*
Tema *Ghana*

Cotonou *Benin*
Port Harcourt *Nigeria*
Douala *Cameroon*
Takoradi *Ghana*
Rotterdam *Holland*
Teesport *United Kingdom*
Hamburg *Germany*

▼ Szczecin *Poland*
A western European port
Dakar *Senegal*
Banjul *Gambia*
Abidjan *Ivory Coast*
Tema *Ghana*

Lomé *Togo*
Cotonou *Benin*
Douala *Cameroon*
Lagos *Nigeria*
A western European port
Szczecin *Poland*

▼ Hamburg *Germany*
Rotterdam *Holland*
Antwerp *Belgium*
Le Havre *France*
Tema *Ghana*
Cotonou *Benin*
Lagos *Nigeria*

Port Harcourt *Nigeria*
Douala *Cameroon*
Takoradi *Ghana*
Rotterdam *Holland*
Teesport *United Kingdom*
Hamburg *Germany*

68 Vega Dania Line, agent: Strand Cruise & Travel, p.208

▼ Dieppe *France*　　　　　　　Dieppe *France*
　 Abidjan *Ivory Coast*

69 St Helena Shipping Company, p.192

▼ Cardiff *United Kingdom*　　　St Helena
　 Tenerife *Canary Islands*　　　Ascension Island
　 Ascension Island　　　　　　 St Helena
　 St Helena　　　　　　　　　Tenerife *Canary Islands*
　 Ascension Island　　　　　　*occasionally*:
　 St Helena　　　　　　　　　Banjul *Gambia*
　 Cape Town *South Africa*　　　Cardiff *United Kingdom*
　 once a year:
　 Tristan da Cunha

70 P&O Containers, p.180

▼ Tilbury *United Kingdom*　　　Port Elizabeth *South Africa*
　 Cape Town *South Africa*　　　Cape Town *South Africa*
　 Port Elizabeth *South Africa*　Tilbury *United Kingdom*
　 Durban *South Africa*

71 Safmarine, p.191

▼ Tilbury *United Kingdom*　　　Zeebrugge *Belgium/*
　 Le Havre *France*　　　　　　　 Le Havre *France*
　 Cape Town *South Africa*　　　Tilbury *United Kingdom*
　 Port Elizabeth/
　　 Durban *South Africa*

72 Baltic Shipping Company, agent: Strand Cruise, p.151

▼ *Northern Route*:
Sydney *Australia*
Brisbane *Australia*
Melbourne *Australia*
Adelaide *Australia*
Fremantle *Australia*
Jeddah *Saudi Arabia*
Suez Canal
Genoa *Italy*
Felixstowe *United Kingdom*

Southern Route:
Felixstowe *United Kingdom*
Durban *South Africa*
Fremantle *Australia*
Melbourne *Australia*
Adelaide *Australia*

73 Mediterranean Shipping Company, p.162

▼ Hamburg *Germany*
Bremen *Germany*
Rotterdam *Holland*
Le Havre *France*
Antwerp *Belgium*
Felixstowe *United Kingdom*
Cape Town *South Africa*

Port Elizabeth *South Africa*
Durban *South Africa*
Cape Town *South Africa*
Le Havre *France*
Antwerp *Belgium*

74 Mediterranean Shipping Company, p.163

▼ Antwerp *Belgium*
Felixstowe *United Kingdom*
Dunkirk *France*
Rouen *France*
Nantes *France*
Pointe-des-Galets *Reunion*

Port-Louis *Mauritius*
Tamatave *Madagascar*
possibly:
Pointe-des-Galets *Reunion*
Antwerp *Belgium*

▼ Livorno *Italy*
Genoa *Italy*
Marseilles *France*
Savona *Italy*
Barcelona *Spain*
Valencia *Spain*
Durban *South Africa*
Pointe-des-Galets *Reunion*

Port-Louis *Mauritius*
Tamatave *Madagascar*
possibly:
Cape Town *South Africa*
Valencia *Spain*
possibly:
Barcelona *Spain*
Livorno *Italy*

▶ Red Sea, East Africa and Indian Ocean Islands

▼ Antwerp *Belgium*
Suez Canal *Egypt*
Hodeïda *Yemen*
Massauo *Ethiopia*
Port Sudan *Sudan*

Jeddah *Saudi Arabia*
Karachi *Pakistan*
Mombasa *Kenya*
Comoros Islands
Antwerp *Belgium*

▼ Hamburg *Germany*
Rotterdam *Holland*
Thamesport *United Kingdom*
Le Havre *France*
Piraeus *Greece*
Suez Canal *Egypt*
Jeddah *Saudi Arabia*
Hodeïda *Yemen*
Aqaba *Jordan*

Yanbu *Saudi Arabia*
Jeddah *Saudi Arabia*
Port Sudan *Sudan*
Suez Canal *Egypt*
Salerno *Italy*
Valencia *Spain*
Thamesport *United Kingdom*
Hamburg *Germany*

▼ Hamburg *Germany*
Rotterdam *Holland*
Le Havre *France*
Piraeus *Greece*
Suez Canal *Egypt*
Jeddah *Saudi Arabia*
Hodeïda *Yemen*
Aqaba *Jordan*

Jeddah *Saudi Arabia*
Port Sudan *Sudan*
Suez Canal *Egypt*
Salerno *Italy*
Valencia *Spain*
Thamesport *United Kingdom*
Hamburg *Germany*

▼ Antwerp *Belgium*
Felixstowe *United Kingdom*
Suez Canal
Djibouti

Dar es Salaam *Tanzania*
Mombasa *Kenya*
Suez Canal
Antwerp *Belgium*

▼ Hamburg *Germany*
Antwerp *Belgium*
Fos-sur-mer *France*
Suez Canal
possibly:
Port Sudan *Sudan*
Djibouti
Dar es Salaam *Tanzania*

Tanga *Tanzania*
Mombasa *Kenya*
possibly:
Djibouti *and* Port Sudan
Suez Canal
Le Havre *France*
Felixstowe *United Kingdom*
Hamburg *Germany*

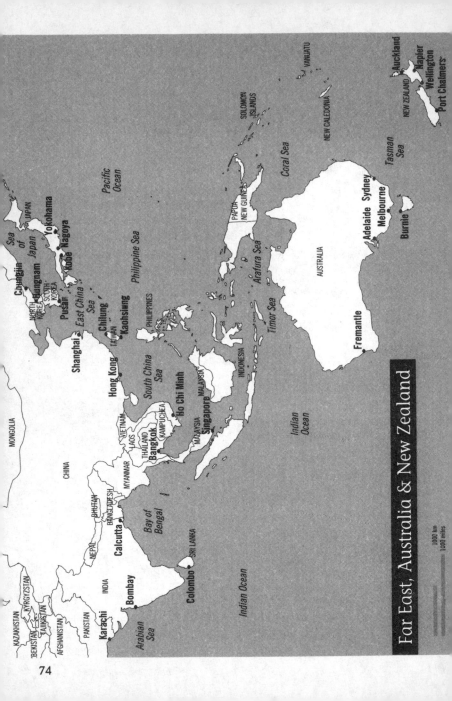

Far East, Australia & New Zealand

▶ Europe

&

▶ India

▶ Asia

▶ The Far East

▶ Australia

▶ New Zealand

▶ Oceania

▶ India

81   N.S.B., p.170

▼ Hamburg *Germany*   Bombay *India*
Antwerp *Belgium*   Suez Canal
Suez Canal   Felixstowe *United Kingdom*
Dubai *United Arab Emirates*   Hamburg *Germany*
Karachi *Pakistan*

82   Nard, agent: Strand Cruise & Travel, p.209

▼ Hamburg *Germany*   Bombay *India*
Felixstowe *United Kingdom*   Colombo *Sri Lanka*
Rotterdam *Holland*   Karachi *Pakistan*
Suez Canal   Suez Canal
Fujairah *United Arab Emirates*   Hamburg *Germany*
Karachi *Pakistan*

▼ Algeciras *Spain*
　Malta
　Suez Canal
　Jeddah *Saudi Arabia*
　Jebel Ali *Sudan*
　Bombay *India*
　Jeddah *Saudi Arabia*
　Suez Canal
　Malta
　Algeciras *Spain*

　Halifax *Canada*
　New York *USA*
　Baltimore *Maryland USA*
　Miami *Florida USA*
　Houston *Texas USA*
　Charleston *South Carolina USA*
　Baltimore *Maryland USA*
　New York *USA*
　Algeciras *Spain*

▶ To Asia, the Far East, Australasia and Oceania

For these destinations, *see also* Round-the-world Voyages, p.91

▼ Bremen *Germany*
　Southampton *United Kingdom*
　Algeciras *Spain*
　Suez Canal
　Jeddah *Saudi Arabia*
　Jebel Ali/Dubai
　　United Arab Emirates
　Hong Kong

　Singapore
　Colombo *Sri Lanka*
　Suez Canal
　Algeciras *Spain*
　Rotterdam *Holland*
　Bremen *Germany*

▼ Bremen *Germany*
  Southampton *United Kingdom*
  Algeciras *Spain*
  Suez Canal
  Jeddah *Saudi Arabia*
  Dubai *United Arab Emirates*
  Hong Kong
  Pusan *South Korea*
  Kaohsiung *Taiwan*

Hong Kong
Singapore
Colombo *Sri Lanka*
Suez Canal
Algeciras *Spain*
Southampton *United Kingdom*
Rotterdam *Holland*
Bremen *Germany*

▼ Hamburg *Germany*
  Zeebrugge *Belgium*
  Southampton *United Kingdom*
  Algeciras *Spain*
  Suez Canal
  Singapore
  Hong Kong
  Kaohsiung *Taiwan*
  Pusan *South Korea*

Kaohsiung *Taiwan*
Hong Kong
Singapore
Suez Canal
Algeciras *Spain*
Southampton *United Kingdom*
Rotterdam *Holland*
Bremen *Germany*
Hamburg *Germany*

▼ Hamburg *Germany*
Rotterdam *Holland*
Felixstowe *United Kingdom*
Le Havre *France*
Malta
Jeddah *Saudi Arabia*
Dubai *United Arab Emirates*
Colombo *Sri Lanka*
Singapore

Hong Kong
Pusan *South Korea*
Keelung (Chilung) *Taiwan*
Hong Kong
Singapore
Colombo *Sri Lanka*
Malta
Algeciras *Spain*
Hamburg *Germany*

▼ Hamburg *Germany*
Isle of Grain *United Kingdom*
Rotterdam *Holland*
Antwerp *Belguim*
Damietta *Egypt*
Jeddah *Saudi Arabia*
Fujairah *United Arab Emirates*
Singapore
Hong Kong

Pusan *South Korea*
Keelung (Chilung) *Taiwan*
Kaohsiung *Taiwan*
Hong Kong
Singapore
Colombo *Sri Lanka*
Damietta *Egypt*
Le Havre *France*
Hamburg *Germany*

▼ Western European ports

Antwerp *Belgium*

Casablanca *Morocco*

Various Mediterranean ports, amongst them:

Marseilles *France*
Genoa *Italy*
Naples *Italy*
La Goulette *Tunisia*
or taking in
Constanza *Black Sea, Romania*

Suez Canal

Singapore

Hong Kong

Various Chinese ports on the Yellow Sea, amongst them:

Shanghai
Huangpu
Lianyungang
Qingdao
Tianjin
Quinghuangdao
Dalian

possibly:
Pusan *South Korea*

Huangnam *North Korea*

Chungjin *North Korea*

(*return voyage via the Mediterranean*)

A western European port

▼ Hamburg *Germany*

Rotterdam *Holland*

Antwerp *Belgium*

Isle of Grain *United Kingdom*

Le Havre *France*

Damietta *Egypt*

Suez Canal

Jeddah *Saudi Arabia*

Fujairah *United Arab Emirates*

Singapore

Hong Kong

Pusan *South Korea*

Keelung (Chilung) *Taiwan*

Kaohsiung *Taiwan*

Hong Kong

Singapore

Colombo *Sri Lanka*

Suez Canal

Damietta *Egypt*

Fos-sur-mer *France*

Barcelona *Spain*

Hamburg *Germany*

▼ La Spezia *Italy*
   Fos-sur-mer *France*
   Suez Canal
   Jeddah *Saudi Arabia*
   Khor Fakkan
     United Arab Emirates
   Singapore

Pusan *South Korea*
Hong Kong
Singapore
Jeddah *Saudi Arabia*
Suez Canal
La Spezia *Italy*

▼ La Spezia *Italy*
   Fos-sur-mer *France*
   Valencia *Spain*
   Larnaka *Cyprus*
   Suez Canal
   Jeddah *Saudi Arabia*
   Khor Fakkan
     United Arab Emirates

Singapore
Pusan *South Korea*
Kaohsiung *Taiwan*
Hong Kong
Singapore
Jeddah *Saudi Arabia*
Suez Canal
La Spezia *Italy*

▼ Hamburg *Germany*
   Gothenburg *Sweden*
   Hamburg *Germany*
   Rotterdam *Holland*
   Southampton *United Kingdom*
   Port Said *Egypt*
   Suez Canal
   Singapore
   Hong Kong
   Pusan *South Korea*
   Shimizu *Japan*

Yokohama *Japan*
Keelung (Chilung) *Taiwan*
Hong Kong
Singapore
Suez Canal
Southampton *United Kingdom*
Rotterdam *Holland*
Hamburg *Germany*
Gothenburg *Sweden*
Hamburg *Germany*

▼ Hamburg *Germany*
  Zeebrugge *Holland*
  Southampton *United Kingdom*
  Algeciras *Spain*
  Malta
  Suez Canal
  Singapore
  Yantian *China*
  Hong Kong

Singapore
Colombo *Sri Lanka*
Jeddah *Saudi Arabia*
Suez Canal
Malta
Algeciras *Spain*
Rotterdam *Holland*
Hamburg *Germany*

▼ Le Havre *France*
  Port Said *Egypt*
  Port Kelang *Malaysia*
  Singapore
  Hong Kong
  Pusan *North Korea*
  Kobe *Japan*

Shimizu *Japan*
Nagoya *Japan*
Yokohama *Japan*
Hong Kong (*second call*)
Singapore (*second call*)
Suez Canal
Le Havre *France*

▼ La Spezia *Italy*
  Barcelona *Spain*
  Fos-sur-mer *France*
  Damietta *Egypt*
  Port Said *Egypt*
  possibly:
  Jeddah *Saudi Arabia*
  Singapore
  Hong Kong
  Pusan *South Korea*

Kobe *Japan*
Nagoya *Japan*
Yokohama *Japan*
Hong Kong (*second call*)
Singapore (*second call*)
Port Kelang *Malaysia*
Suez Canal
Damietta *Egypt*
La Spezia *Italy*

▼ Hamburg *Germany*
Rotterdam *Holland*
La Spezia *Italy*
Suez Canal
Melbourne *Australia*
Fremantle *Australia*

Suez Canal
La Spezia *Italy*
Zeebrugge *Belgium*
Tilbury *United Kingdom*
Hamburg *Germany*

▼ Hamburg *Germany*
Rotterdam *Holland*
Barcelona *Spain*
La Spezia *Italy*
Suez Canal
Melbourne *Australia*
Sydney *Australia*

Melbourne *Australia*
Fremantle *Australia*
Suez Canal
La Spezia *Italy*
Zeebrugge *Belgium*
Tilbury *United Kingdom*

▼ Tilbury *United Kingdom*
Rotterdam *Holland*
Cape Town *South Africa*
Fremantle *Australia*
Adelaide *Australia*
Burnie *Australia*
Melbourne *Australia*
Sydney *Australia*

Auckland *New Zealand*
Wellington *New Zealand*
Lyttleton *New Zealand*
Port Chalmers *New Zealand*
Lisbon *Portugal*
Zeebrugge *Belgium*
Tilbury *United Kingdom*

▼ Felixstowe *United Kingdom*
  Durban *South Africa*
  possibly:
  Fremantle *Australia*
  Melbourne *Australia*
  Sydney *Australia*

  possibly:
  Adelaide *Australia*
  Fremantle *Australia*
  Jeddah *Saudi Arabia*
  Suez Canal
  Genoa *Italy*
  Felixstowe *United Kingdom*

▼ Le Havre *France*
  Antwerp *Belgium*
  Felixstowe *United Kingdom*
  Cape Town *South Africa*
  Port Elizabeth *South Africa*
  Durban *South Africa*
  Fremantle *Australia*
  Sydney *Australia*

  Melbourne *Australia*
  every other week:
  Adelaide *Australia*
  Fremantle *Australia*
  Durban *South Africa*
  Port Elizabeth *South Africa*
  Cape Town *South Africa*
  Le Havre *France*

▼ Salerno *Italy*
  La Spezia *Italy*
  Fos-sur-mer *France*
  Barcelona *Spain*
  Piraeus *Greece*
  Suez Canal
  Jeddah *Saudi Arabia*
  Fremantle *Australia*
  Melbourne *Australia*
  Sydney *Australia*
  Auckland *New Zealand*

  Wellington *New Zealand*
  Port Chalmers *New Zealand*
  Melbourne *Australia*
  Fremantle *Australia*
  Jeddah *Saudi Arabia*
  Suez Canal
  Piraeus *Greece*
  Barcelona *Spain*
  Fos-sur-mer *France*
  La Spezia *Italy*
  Salerno *Italy*

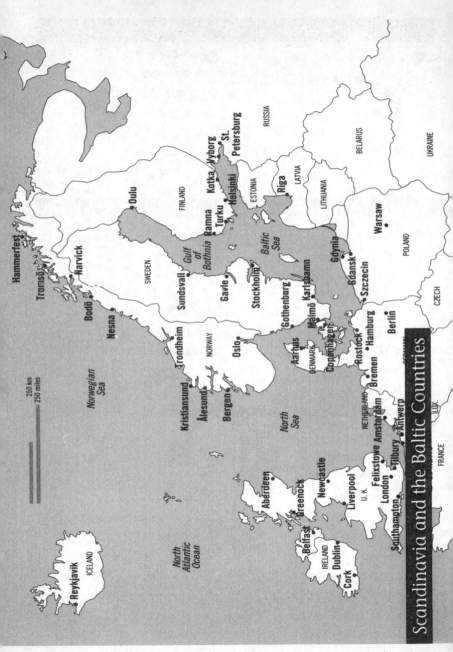

Scandinavia and the Baltic Countries

84

▶ **Europe**

&

▶ **Scandinavia**

▶ **The Baltic Countries**

103　　　　　　　　　　　　　　　　　**Hurtigruten, p.146**

▼ *Voyage along the Norwegian coastline*:

Bergen

Florø

Måløy

Torvik

Ålesund

Molde

Kristiansund

Trondheim

Rorvik

Brønnøysund

Sandnessjøen

Nesna

Ørnes

Bodø

Lofoten Islands:
  Stamsund, Svolvaer,
  Stokmarknes, Sortland,
  Risoyhamn, Harstad

Finnsnes

Tromsø

Skjervoy

Oksfjord

Alta

Hammerfest

Havoysund

Honningsvag

Kjollefjord

Mehamn

Berlevag

Batsfjord

Vardo

Vadsø

Kirkenes

Bergen

104   Icelandic Steamship Company, p.149

▼ Immingham *United Kingdom*   Hamburg *Germany*
Reykjavik *Iceland*   Rotterdam *Holland*
Immingham *United Kingdom*   Immingham *United Kingdom*

105   Reederei Russ, agent: Strand Cruise & Travel, p.210

▼ A western European port   Rauma *Finland*
Kotka *Finland*   Oulu *Finland*
Hamina *Finland*   A western European port
Hanko *Finland*

106   M. Schiffahrts, agent: Strand Cruise & Travel, p.211

▼ Hamburg *Germany*
Ports in Norway:
  Oslo
  Moss
  Kristiansand
Ports in Sweden:
  Gothenburg
  Halmstadt
  Stockholm
  Gävle
  Norrköping
  Karlshamn

Ports in Finland:
  Helsinki
  Hanko
  Rauma
  Turku
  Mäntilouto
Ports in Poland:
  Gdynia
  Szczecin
Ports in Belgium:
  Antwerp
  Zeebrugge
Hamburg *Germany*

107   Parten, agent: Strand Cruise & Travel, p.211

▼ Hamburg *Germany*   Norway
Kiel Canal   Kiel Canal
Ports in Sweden   Hamburg *Germany*
Finland

▼ Antwerp *Belgium*/   Hamina *Finland*
    Amsterdam *Holland*   Amsterdam *Holland*/
   Turku *Finland*   Antwerp *Belgium*
   Helsinki *Finland*

▼ Emden *Germany*   Ports in Finland:
   Helgoland Islands *Germany*   Helsinki
   Kiel Canal   Kotka
   Fredericia *Denmark*   Hamina
   Horsens *Denmark*   Saimaaseen
   Køge *Denmark*   Vyborg *Russia*
        A port in Germany

▼ Felixstowe *United Kingdom*   Kotka *Finland*
   Vlissingen *Holland*   Hamburg *Germany*
   Hamburg *Germany*   Rotterdam *Holland*
   St Petersburg *Russia*   Felixstowe *United Kingdom*

▼ Bremen *Germany*   *or else*:
   Aarhus *Denmark*   Hamburg *Germany*
   Gothenburg *Sweden*   Kiel Canal
   Helsinborg *Sweden*   Helsinki *Finland*
   Malmö *Sweden*   Kotka *Finland*
        A port in Germany

112 — Agent: Hamburger Abendblatt/Die Welt, p.225

▼ Rotterdam *Holland*
(via the Skagerrak Straits)
Helsinki *Finland*

Teesport *United Kingdom*
Rotterdam *Holland*

113 — Reederei Ritscher, agent: Strand Cruise & Travel, p.212

▼ Rotterdam *Holland*
Kiel Canal
Helsinki *Finland*
St Petersburg *Russia*
Helsinki *Finland*

possibly:
Aarhus *Denmark*
Kiel Canal
Bremen *Germany*
Rotterdam *Holland*

114 — North Navigation, agent: Strand Cruise & Travel, p.212

▼ Kiel *Germany*
Antwerp *Belgium*
Kiel *Germany*

Skölvig *Finland*
Kiel *Germany*

115 — Agent: Hamburg-Süd, p.219

▼ A port in Germany
Sweden

Denmark
A port in Germany

116 — Agent: Strand Cruise & Travel, p.212

▼ Hamburg *Germany*
Bremen *Germany*
possibly:
Oslo *Norway*
Gothenburg *Sweden*

Copenhagen *Denmark*
Malmö *Sweden*
Helsingborg *Sweden*
Kiel Canal
Hamburg *Germany*

117   J. Kahrs, agent: Strand Cruise & Travel, p.213

▼ Hamburg *Germany*

Kiel Canal

Copenhagen *Denmark*
or Helsinborg *Sweden*
or Malmö *Sweden*

Gothenburg *Sweden*

Copenhagen *Denmark*
or Helsinborg *Sweden*
or Malmö *Sweden*

Kiel Canal

Bremen *Germany*

Hamburg *Germany*

118   Reederei Speck, agent: Strand Cruise & Travel, p.213

▼ Hamburg *Germany*

Bremen *Germany*

Oslo *Norway*
or Gothenburg *Sweden*

Aarhus *Denmark*

Ports in Denmark or Sweden

Kiel Canal

Hamburg *Germany*

119   Agent: Frachtschiff-Touristik, p.213

▼ Kiel *Germany*

Goole (River Humber)
United Kingdom

A port in Sweden,
*with various ports of call
on the Mälaren Sea,*

occasionally as far as
Västeras *Sweden*

Kiel *Germany*

120   M. Schiffahrts, agent: Strand Cruise & Travel, p.214

▼ Hamburg *Germany*

Kiel Canal

Gdynia *Poland*

Kiel Canal

Bremen *Germany*

Hamburg *Germany*

121   Polish Ocean Lines, p.187

▼ Felixstowe *United Kingdom*

Copenhagen *Denmark*

Gdynia *Poland*

Copenhagen *Denmark*

Felixstowe *United Kingdom*

122   West Navigation, agent: Strand Cruise & Travel, p.214

▼ Kiel *Germany*
   Aarhus *Denmark*
   Riga *Latvia*
   Kiel Canal
   Tilbury *United Kingdom*

possibly:
Rotterdam *Holland*
or Antwerp *Belgium*
Kiel *Germany*

123   Reederei U. Salge, agent: Strand Cruise & Travel, p.214

▼ Hamburg/Stadersand *Germany*
   Rotterdam *Holland*
   Dublin *Ireland*
   Belfast *Northern Ireland*
   Cork *Ireland*

Southampton *United Kingdom*
Le Havre *France*
Antwerp *Belgium*
Hamburg *Germany*

124   Caribic Navigation, agent: Strand Cruise & Travel, p.215

▼ Antwerp *Belgium*
   Dublin *Ireland*

Le Havre *France*
Antwerp *Belgium*

125   Reederei U. Jess, agent: Strand Cruise & Travel, p.215

▼ Le Havre *France*
   Southampton *United Kingdom*
   Dublin *Ireland*
   Belfast *Northern Ireland*

Greenock *United Kingdom*
Southampton *United Kingdom*
Le Havre *France*

126   Agent: Hamburg-Süd, p.220

▼ Rotterdam *Holland*
   Cork *Ireland*
   Dublin *Ireland*

Belfast *Northern Ireland*
Rotterdam *Holland*

▶ Westwards Round the World

127 N.S.B., p.175

Hamburg *Germany*
Rotterdam *Holland*
Dunkirk *France*
Le Havre *France*
New York *USA*
Norfolk *Virginia USA*
Savannah *Georgia USA*
Panama Canal
Papeete *Tahiti*
Noumea *New Caledonia*
Auckland *New Zealand*
Melbourne *Australia*
Sydney *Australia*
Keelung *Taiwan*
Hong Kong
Singapore
Suez Canal
Port Said *Egypt*
Salerno *Italy*
Savona *Italy*
Felixstowe *United Kingdom*
Hamburg *Germany*

128 N.S.B., p.175

Hamburg *Germany*
Rotterdam *Holland*
Barcelona *Spain*
Fos-sur-mer *France*
Suez Canal
Melbourne *Australia*
Sydney *Australia*
Auckland *New Zealand*
Keelung *Taiwan*
Hong Kong
Singapore
Suez Canal
Port Said *Egypt*
Salerno *Italy*
Savona *Italy*
Felixstowe *United Kingdom*
Hamburg *Germany*

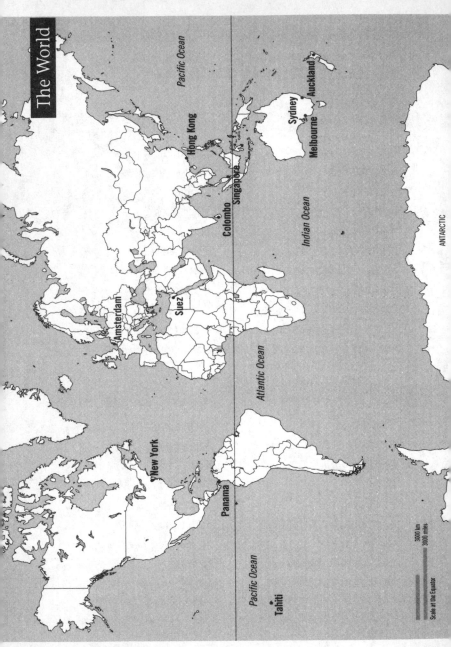

The World

Pacific Ocean

Hong Kong

Auckland

Sydney

Melbourne

Singapore

Colombo

Indian Ocean

Amsterdam

Suez

ANTARCTIC

Atlantic Ocean

New York

Panama

Pacific Ocean

Tahiti

3000 km
3000 miles

Scale at the Equator

▼ Hamburg *Germany*
   Hull *United Kingdom*
   Antwerp *Belgium*
   Dunkirk *France*
   Le Havre *France*
   Panama Canal
   Papeete *Tahiti*
   possibly:
   Apia *Samoa*
   Suva *Fiji*
   Lautoka *Fiji*
   Noumea *New Caledonia*
   Port Vila *Vanuatu*
   Santo *Vanuatu*

Honiara *Solomon Islands*
Yandina *Solomon Islands*
Lae *Papua New Guinea*
Madang *Papua New Guinea*
Kimbe *Papua New Guinea*
Rabaul *Papua New Guinea*
Darwin *Australia*
Singapore
Suez Canal
Antwerp *Belguim*
Rotterdam *Holland*
Hamburg *Germany*
Hull *United Kingdom*

▼ Le Havre *France*
   Savannah *Georgia USA*
   Cristobal *Panama*
   Papeete *Tahiti*
   possibly:
   Don Iambo *Mururoa*
   Noumea *New Caledonia*
   Melbourne *Australia*
   Sydney *Australia*

Brisbane *Australia*
Lae *Papua New Guinea*
Jakarta *Indonesia*
Colombo *Sri Lanka*
Suez Canal
Genoa *Italy*
Marseilles *France*

▶ Eastwards Round the World

131   ABC Containerline, p.112

▼ Liverpool *United Kingdom*   Auckland *New Zealand*
    Zeebrugge *Belgium*   Lyttleton *New Zealand*
    Haifa *Israel*   Panama Canal
    Suez Canal   US Gulfport
    Singapore   New Orleans *Louisiana USA*
    Geraldton *Australia*   Charleston *South Carolina USA*
    Fremantle *Australia*   Philadelphia *Pennsylvania USA*
    Melbourne *Australia*   Halifax *Canada*
    Sydney *Australia*   Liverpool *United Kingdom*

132   N.S.B., p.176

▼ Hamburg *Germany*   Kobe *Japan*
    Felixstowe *United Kingdom*   Pusan *South Korea*
    Rotterdam *Holland*   Kaohsiung *Taiwan*
    Port Said *Egypt*   Hong Kong
    Suez Canal   Singapore
    Singapore   Suez Canal
    Hong Kong   Port Said *Egypt*
    Kaohsiung *Taiwan*   Rotterdam *Holland*
    Yokohama *Japan*   Hamburg *Germany*

Ports of Registry in:
▶ **The American Continent**
▶ **The Caribbean**

The port of registry, from which the boat leaves and returns, is only a geographical pointer. It does not imply that this is the port of departure.

▶ **South America**

133	Ivaran Lines, p.150

▼ New Orleans *Louisiana USA*
Houston *Texas USA*
Puerto Cabello *Venezuela*
La Guaira *Venezuela*
Rio de Janeiro *Brazil*
Santos *Brazil*
Buenos Aires *Argentina*
Montevideo *Uruguay*
Rio Grande *Brazil*
Itajai *Brazil*

Santos *Brazil*
Rio de Janeiro *Brazil*
possibly:
Salvador/Fortaleza *Brazil*
Bridgetown *Barbados*
San Juan *Puerto Rico*
Veracruz *Mexico*
Altamira *Mexico*
New Orleans *Louisiana USA*

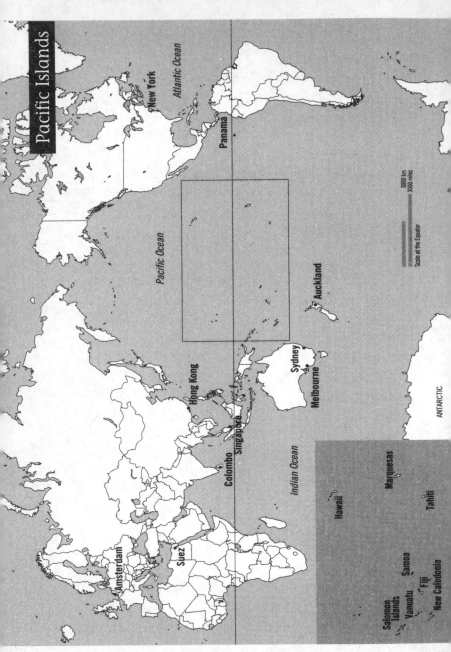

Pacific Islands

New York

Atlantic Ocean

Panama

Pacific Ocean

Auckland

Sydney

Hong Kong

Melbourne

Singapore

Colombo

Indian Ocean

Amsterdam

Suez

ANTARCTIC

Hawaii

Marquesas

Tahiti

Solomon
Islands

Vanuatu

Samoa

Fiji

New Caledonia

3000 km
3000 miles

Scale at the Equator

▼ New Orleans *Louisiana USA*
Houston *Texas USA*
Puerto Cabello *Venezuela*
La Guaira *Venezuela*
Recife Brazil
Rio de Janeiro *Brazil*
Santos *Brazil*
Buenos Aires *Argentina*
Montevideo *Uruguay*
Rio Grande *Brazil*

Itajai *Brazil*
Paranagua *Brazil*
Santos *Brazil*
Fortaleza *Brazil*
Salvador *Brazil*
San Juan *Puerto Rico*
Veracruz *Mexico*
Tampico *Mexico*
New Orleans *Louisiana USA*
Houston *Texas USA*

▼ Port Elizabeth *New Jersey USA*
Baltimore *Maryland USA*
Norfolk *Virginia USA*
Savannah *Georgia USA*
Miami *Florida USA*
Puerto Cabello *Venezuela*
La Guaira *Venezuela*
Rio de Janeiro *Brazil*
Santos *Brazil*

Buenos Aires *Argentina*
Montevideo *Uruguay*
Rio Grande *Brazil*
Itajai *Brazil*
Santos *Brazil*
Rio de Janeiro *Brazil*
possibly:
Salvador/Fortaleza *Brazil*
Port Elizabeth *New Jersey USA*

▼ New York *USA*
Philadelphia *Pennsylvania USA*
Baltimore *Maryland USA*
Norfolk *Virginia USA*
Jacksonville *Florida USA*
Miami *Florida USA*
Fort-de-France *Martinique*
Bridgetown *Barbados*
Port of Spain *Trinidad*
Rio de Janeiro *Brazil*
Santos *Brazil*

Buenos Aires *Argentina*
Montevideo *Uruguay*
Imbituba *Brazil*
Itajai *Brazil*
Sao Francisco do Sul *Brazil*
Santos *Brazil*
Rio de Janeiro *Brazil*
Salvador *Brazil*
Recife *Brazil*
Fortaleza *Brazil*
New York *USA*

▼ Miami *Florida USA*
Aruba *Curaçao*
Puerto Cabello *Venezuela*

La Guaira *Venezuela*
Miami *Florida USA*

▼ Savannah *Georgia USA*
Fernandina Beach *Florida USA*
Santos *Brazil*
Buenos Aires *Argentina*
Montevideo *Uruguay*

Rio Grande *Brazil*
Santos *Brazil*
possibly:
Vitoria *Brazil*
Norfolk *Virginia USA*

139 — Lykes Line, p.155

▼ A port in the Gulf of Mexico *USA*
Colombia
Panama
Peru
Ecuador
Chile
USA

140 — Kahrs Line, agent: Freighter World Cruises, p.217

▼ Long Beach *California USA*
Puerto Quetzal *Guatemala*
Balboa *Panama*
Puerto Caldera *Costa Rica*
Acajutla *El Salvador*
Long Beach *California USA*

141 — C.G.M., p.126

▼ *Inter-island voyages between Martinique and Puerto Rico*:
Pointe-à-Pitre *Martinique*
St Kitts (*1 call in 3*)
Antigua/St Barthélémy/St Martin
San Juan *Puerto Rico*
St Martin
Montserrat
Pointe-à-Pitre *Martinique*

142 — Armada Argentina, p.114

▼ *Voyage along the Argentinian coastline*:
Buenos Aires *Argentina*
Deseado *Argentina*
San Julian *Argentina*
Ushuaia *Argentina*
Port Stanley *Falkland Islands*
Buenos Aires *Argentina*

143 — Navimag, p.168

▼ *Voyage along the Chilean coastline*:
Puerto Montt *Chile*
Puerto Natales *Chile*

South Pacific

144   Blue Star Line, p.120

▼ Jacksonville *Florida USA*
or a port on the east coast of the USA:
Philadelphia, Norfolk *or* Houston
Panama
Melbourne *Australia*
Sydney *Australia*
Brisbane *Australia*

possibly:
Port Chalmers *New Zealand*
Wellington *New Zealand*
Auckland *New Zealand*
Panama
Philadelphia *Pennsylvania USA*

145   Columbus Line, p.122

▼ Jacksonville *Florida USA*
Houston *Texas USA*
Panama Canal
possibly:
Auckland *New Zealand*
Melbourne *Australia*
Sydney *Australia*
possibly:
Brisbane *Australia*

possibly:
Port Chalmers *New Zealand*
Wellington *New Zealand*
Auckland *New Zealand*
Panama Canal
possibly:
Kingston *Jamaica*
Philadelphia *Pennsylvania USA*

146   Blue Star Line, p.120

▼ Los Angeles *California USA*
Auckland *New Zealand*
Sydney *Australia*
Melbourne *Australia*
Wellington *New Zealand*

Auckland *New Zealand*
Suva *Fiji*
Seattle *Washington USA*
Los Angeles *California USA*

▼ Los Angeles *California USA*   Auckland *New Zealand*
  Auckland *New Zealand*   *occasionally*:
  Sydney *Australia*   Honolulu *Hawaii*
  Melbourne *Australia*   Seattle *Washington USA*
  Wellington *New Zealand*   Los Angeles *California USA*

▶ Asia

▼ A port in the Gulf of Mexico, *USA*   Thailand
  Manila *Philippines*   China
  Indonesia   Japan
  Malaysia   Hong Kong
  occasionally: Gulf of Mexico *USA*
  Singapore

▼ Vancouver *BC Canada*   Nagoya *Japan*
  Seattle *Washington USA*   Shimizu *Japan*
  Tomakomai *Japan*   Tokyo *Japan*
  Pusan *South Korea*   Seattle *Washington USA*
  Kobe *Japan*   Vancouver *BC Canada*

▼ Esmeraldas *Ecuador*
  Arica *Chile*
  Iquique *Chile*
  Valparaiso *Chile*
  Chonoral *Chile*
  Antofagasta *Chile*
  Ilo *Peru*
  Callao *Peru*
  Yokohama *Japan*
  Onahama *Japan*

Nagoya *Japan*
Kobe *Japan*
Pusan *South Korea*
Keelung *Taiwan*
Hong Kong
Pusan *South Korea*
Hiroshima *Japan*
Kobe *Japan*
Esmeraldas *Ecuador*

▶ # Africa

▼ Charleston *South Carolina USA*
  Norfolk *Virginia USA*
  Baltimore *Maryland USA*
  New York *USA*

Cape Town *South Africa*
Durban *South Africa*
Cape Town *South Africa*
Charleston *South Carolina USA*

▼ A port in the Gulf of Mexico *USA*
  Cape Town *South Africa*
  Port Elizabeth *South Africa*
  East London *South Africa*
  Durban *South Africa*

Maputo *Mozambique*
Beira *Mozambique*
Dar es Salaam *Tanzania*
Mombasa *Kenya*
Gulf of Mexico *USA*

▼ Savannah *Georgia USA*
Newport News *Virginia USA*
Baltimore *Maryland USA*
Canary Islands
Dakar *Senegal*
Abidjan *Ivory Coast*
Cape Town *South Africa*
Durban *South Africa*

Cape Town *South Africa*
Recife *Brazil*
La Guaira *Venezuela*
San Juan *Puerto Rico*
Veracruz *Mexico*
Houston *Texas USA*
New Orleans *Louisiana USA*
Savannah *Georgia USA*

▼ Puerto Caldera *Costa Rica*
Manta *Ecuador*
Chile
Peru
Manta *Ecuador*
Buenaventura *Colombia*
Puerto Caldera *Costa Rica*
Japan

Taiwan
Hong Kong
Singapore
Korea
Japan
Lazaro Cardenas *Mexico*
Puerto Caldera *Costa Rica*

▼ *Voyage along the east coast of Canada*:

Rimouski
Sept-Iles
Port Menier (Ile d'Anticosti)
Havre-St-Pierre
Baie Johan Beetz
Natashquan
Kegashka
La Romaine
Harrington Harbour
Tête-à-la-Baleine
La Tabatière
St Augustin
Vieux-Fort

Blanc-Sablon
Vieux-Fort
St Augustin
La Tabatière
Tête-à-la-Baleine
Harrington Harbour
La Romaine
Kegashka
Natashquan
Baie Johan Beets
Havre-St-Pierre
Port-Menier
Sept-Iles
Rimouski

Ports of Registry in:
▶ **Africa**
▶ **Mauritius**

156 — Unicorn Lines, p.195

▼ Durban *South Africa*   Cape Town *South Africa*
  Cape Town *South Africa*   East London *South Africa*
  Walvis Bay *Namibia*   Durban *South Africa*

157 — Unicorn Lines, p.196

▼ Durban *South Africa*   Bombay *India*
  Nacala *Mozambique*   Mombasa *Kenya*
  Dar es Salaam *Tanzania*   Dar es Salaam *Tanzania*
  Mombasa *Kenya*   Nacala *Mozambique*
  Karachi *Pakistan*   Durban *South Africa*
  Dubai *United Arab Emirates*

158 — Mediterranean Shipping Company, p.165

▼ Durban *South Africa*   *possibly*:
  Port-Louis *Mauritius*   Mayotte *Comoros Islands*
  Pointe-des-Galets *Reunion*   Tamatave *Madagascar*
                                 Durban *South Africa*

159 — Mauritius Shipping Corporation, p.158

▼ Port-Louis *Mauritius*   Agalega Islands
  Port-Mathurin *Rodriguez Island*   Ports in Madagascar
  occasionally other ports   Seychelles
  in the Indian Ocean: *and occasionally*:
  Pointe-des-Galets *Reunion*   South Africa

Ports of Registry in:
▶ The Far East
▶ Australasia
▶ Oceania

| 160 | Egon Oldendorff, p.139 |

▼ Singapore
Jebel Ali *United Arab Emirates*
Dammam *United Arab Emirates*
Singapore
Yokohama *Japan*

Kobe *Japan*
Pusan *South Korea*
Keelung *Taiwan*
Shekou *Hong Kong*
Singapore

| 161 | N.S.B., p.177 |

▼ Singapore
Hong Kong
Keelung *Taiwan*
Pusan *South Korea*
Kobe *Japan*
Yokohama *Japan*
Lazaro Cardenas *Mexico*
Manta *Ecuador*
Callao *Peru*
Iquique *Chile*
San Antonio *Chile*

Arica *Peru*
Callao *Peru*
Manta *Ecuador*
Buenaventura *Colombia*
Puerto Caldera *Chile*
Yokohama *Japan*
Kobe *Japan*
Pusan *South Korea*
Keelung *Taiwan*
Hong Kong
Singapore

▼ Pusan *South Korea*   Seattle *Washington USA*
Hong Kong   Portland *Oregon USA*
Kaohsiung *Taiwan*   Seattle *Washington USA*
Pusan *South Korea*   Pusan *South Korea*

▼ Pusan *South Korea*   Santos *Brazil*
Keelung *Taiwan*   Salvador *Brazil*
Hong Kong   Durban *South Africa*
Singapore   Singapore
Buenos Aires *Argentina*   Manila *Philippines*
Montevideo *Uruguay*   Hong Kong
Rio Grande *Brazil*   Keelung *Taiwan*
Sao Francisco do Sul *Brazil*   Pusan *South Korea*
Paranagua *Brazil*

▼ Pusan *South Korea*
Kobe *Japan*
Yokohama *Japan*
Lazaro Cardenas *Mexico*
Callao *Peru*
Iquique *Chile*
San Antonio *Chile*
Arica *Peru*
Ilo *Peru*
Callao *Peru*
Manta *Ecuador*
Buenaventura *Colombia*
Yokohama *Japan*
Nagoya *Japan*
Kobe *Japan*
Pusan *South Korea*
Keelung *Taiwan*

Hong Kong
Singapore
Durban *South Africa*
Cape Town *South Africa*
Montevideo *Uruguay*
Buenos Aires *Argentina*
Sao Francisco do Sul *Brazil*
Paranagua *Brazil*
Santos *Brazil*
Vitoria *Brazil*
Durban *South Africa*
Colombo *Sri Lanka*
Singapore
Hong Kong
Keelung *Taiwan*
Pusan *South Korea*

▼ Hong Kong
Keelung *Taiwan*
Pusan *South Korea*
Hiroshima *Japan*
Osaka *Japan*
Nagoya *Japan*
Yokohama *Japan*
Suva *Fiji*
or Noumea *New Caledonia*

Auckland *New Zealand*
Napier *New Zealand*
Nelson *New Zealand*
Timaru *New Zealand*
Tauranga *New Zealand*
Suva *Fiji*
or Noumea *New Caledonia*
Manila *Philippines*
Hong Kong

166 — Egon Oldendorff, p.140

▼ Auckland *New Zealand*
Lyttleton *New Zealand*
Port Chalmers *New Zealand*
Napier *New Zealand*
Tauranga *New Zealand*
Surabaya *Indonesia*
Jakarta *Indonesia*

Port Kelang *Malaysia*
Singapore
Bangkok *Thailand*
Singapore
Noumea *New Caledonia*
Suva *Fiji*
Auckland *New Zealand*

167 — Egon Oldendorff, p.140

▼ Sydney *Australia*
Melbourne *Australia*
Brisbane *Australia*
Yokohama *Japan*
Osaka *Japan*

Pusan *South Korea*
Sydney *Australia*
Melbourne *Australia*
Brisbane *Australia*

168 — Mediterranean Shipping Company, p.165

▼ Durban *South Africa*
Fremantle *Australia*
Sydney *Australia*
Melbourne *Australia*

every other week:
Adelaide *Australia*
Fremantle *Australia*
Durban *South Africa*

169 — Palau Shipping Company, p.181

▼ *Inter-island voyages in Micronesia*:
Koror *Palau Islands*

Yap
Guam *Mariana Islands*
Koror *Palau Islands*

Inter-island voyages between Tahiti and Bora Bora:

Papeete *Tahiti*

Various neighbouring islands in French Polynesia:

Huahine

Raiatea

Tahaa

Bora Bora

Papeete

Bora Bora

Tahaa

Raiatea

Huahine

Papeete

Inter-island voyages between Tahiti and the Marquesas Islands:

Papeete *Tahiti*

Takapoto *Tuamotou*

Ua Pou, Nuku Hiva, Hiva Oa, Fatu Hiva, Hiva Oa, Ua Huka, Nuku Hiva *Marquesas Islands*

Rangiroa *Tuamotou*

Papeete *Tahiti*

Shipping Companies

ABC Containers

Agent in UK:

> The Strand Cruise and Travel Centre
> Charing Cross Shopping Concourse
> The Strand
> London WC2N 4HZ United Kingdom
> ✆ (0171) 836 6363, 🖷 (0171) 497 0078 (international code: 44)

This Belgian company offers cabins on five container ships sailing eastwards round the world via the Suez Canal (contrary to most round-the-world lines which generally go westwards). Each vessel has three types of grading: deluxe, cabin and economy class. Deluxe means that all cabins are fitted with TV and refridgerator and are of a very high standard; cabin means that while accommodation is of a high standard, there is no TV or refrigerator in the cabins; economy means that while cabins are comfortable they are very basically fitted out.

> **Nationalities:** Belgian officers, international crew
>
> **Conditions:** maximum age 80

Itinerary

Round trip: about 100 days

131 ▼ Liverpool *United Kingdom*
Zeebrugge *Belgium*
Haifa *Israel*
Suez Canal
Singapore
Geraldton *Australia*
Fremantle *Australia*
Melbourne *Australia*
Sydney *Australia*

Auckland *New Zealand*
Lyttleton *New Zealand*
Panama Canal
US Gulfport
New Orleans *Louisiana USA*
Charleston *South Carolina USA*
Philadelphia *New Jersey USA*
Halifax *Canada*
Liverpool *United Kingdom*

Ships and Fares

Ellen Hudig

> Deluxe class, built in 1983, 42,077 tons, 9 passengers, 4 twin cabins, 1 single cabin.
>
> **Facilities:** Cabins with shower/wc, TV, refrigerator; video lounge, bar, gym, pool

Round trip: £7000 to £8500, or £70 to £85 per day

Liverpool	▶	Fremantle	36 days	£2750/£3260
Fremantle	▶	Liverpool	64 days	£4680/£5440
Liverpool	▶	Sydney	44 days	£3300/£3740
Sydney	▶	Liverpool	56 days	£4200/£4760
Liverpool	▶	Auckland	50 days	£3750/£4250
Auckland	▶	Liverpool	50 days	£3750/£4250

Martha II

Cabin class, built in 1984, 41,151 tons, 3 passengers, 3 single cabins

Round trip: £7000, or £70 per day

Liverpool	▶	Fremantle	36 days	£2750
Fremantle	▶	Liverpool	64 days	£4040
Liverpool	▶	Sydney	44 days	£3300
Sydney	▶	Liverpool	56 days	£3640
Liverpool	▶	Auckland	50 days	£3750
Auckland	▶	Liverpool	50 days	£3250

Cornelis Verolme

Economy class, built in 1983, 42,077 tons, 4 passengers, one twin cabin, 2 single cabins

Facilities: cabins with shower/wc, video lounge, gym, pool

Round trip: £6000, or £60 per day

Liverpool	▶	Fremantle	36 days	£2360
Fremantle	▶	Liverpool	64 days	£4040
Liverpool	▶	Sydney	44 days	£2860
Sydney	▶	Liverpool	56 days	£3640
Liverpool	▶	Auckland	50 days	£3250
Auckland	▶	Liverpool	50 days	£3250

Brussel

Economy class, built in 1979, 41,078 tons, 2 passengers, 2 single cabins

Facilities: cabins with shower/wc, video lounge, pool

Antwerpen

Economy class, built in 1979, 41,078 tons, 2 passengers, 2 single cabins

Facilities: cabins with shower/wc, video lounge, pool

Armada Argentina

3 Piso, Avenida Corrientes 389
Buenos Aires, Argentina

This Argentinian company offers trips from Buenos Aires to Tierra del Fuego and the Falkland Islands on board the passenger-cargo ship **Bahia Buen Sucesso**, which can accommodate 60 passengers.

Itinerary

142 ▼ *Voyage along the Argentinian coastline*:
Buenos Aires *Argentina*
Deseado *Argentina*
San Julian *Argentina*
Ushuaia *Argentina*
Port Stanley *Falkland Islands*
Buenos Aires *Argentina*

Fares: on demand

Monthly service from Buenos Aires to Ushuaia; quarterly service to Port Stanley.

Baltic Shipping Company

Agent in UK:

The Strand Cruise and Travel Centre
Charing Cross Shopping Concourse
The Strand
London WC2N 4HZ United Kingdom
✆ (0171) 836 6363, ✇ (0171) 497 0078 (international code: 44)

A Russian shipping company based in St Petersburg, whose vessels sail in the Baltic and in the South Pacific, and which is beginning to welcome passengers on board. Passengers should be warned that conditions are very basic.

Nationalities: Russian officers and crew
Conditions: maximum age 80

Ships

Pyotr Masherov
> Built in 1982, 29,500 tons, 6 passengers, 3 twin cabins

Skulptor Zalkasn
> Built in 1978, 29,500 tons, 6 passengers, 3 twin cabins

Anatoliyi Vasiljev
> Built in 1981, 37,500 tons, 6 passengers, 3 twin cabins

Akademik Gorbunov
> Built in 1986, 29,500 tons, 12 passengers, 6 twin cabins

Smolensk
> Built in 1981, 37,500 tons, 8 passengers, 4 twin cabins

Skultor Konenkov
> Built in 1975, 29,500 tons, 6 passengers, 3 twin cabins

Magnitogorsk
> Built in 1976, 37,500 tons, 8 passengers, 4 twin cabins

Georgiy Pyasetskiy
> Built in 1982, 29,500 tons, 6 passengers, 3 twin cabins

Facilities: all vessels have video lounge, gym, pool, and often a doctor on board.

Itinerary

Duration: 31–39 days

72/ ▼ Felixstowe *United Kingdom*   Sydney *Australia*
100   Durban *South Africa*   *possibly*: Brisbane *Australia*
       possibly: Fremantle *Australia*   Adelaide *Australia*

Fares

Felixstowe	▶	Fremantle	31 days	£1550/£1938
or £50 to £62 per day				
Felixstowe	▶	Sydney	35 days	£1750/£2188
Felixstowe	▶	Brisbane	37 days	£1850/£2313

The return journey from Australia goes via: Jeddah *Saudi Arabia*–Suez Canal–Genoa, *Italy*–Felixstowe, *United Kingdom*
(Duration: 29–42 days)

Sydney	▶	Felixstowe	42 days	£2000/£2500
Melbourne	▶	Felixstowe	36 days	£1800/£2250
Fremantle	▶	Felixstowe	29 days	£1450/£1813

Itinerary

Round trip: about 22 days

110 ▼ Felixstowe *United Kingdom* Kotka *Finland*
Vlissingen *Holland* Hamburg *Germany*
Hamburg *Germany* Rotterdam *Holland*
St Petersburg *Russia* Felixstowe *United Kingdom*

Fares

Round trip: about £1450 to £1815, or £65 to £82 per day
This fare includes a stay of 4 to 7 days in one of St Petersburg's premier hotels.

Bank Line

Dexter House
2 Royal Mint Court,
London EC3N 4XX United Kingdom
✆ (0171) 265 0808, ✆ (0171) 481 4784 (international code: 44)

Agent in USA:

Freighter World Cruises
180 South Lake Avenue, Suite 335
Pasadena
California 91101 USA
✆ (818) 449 31 06, ✆ (818) 449 95 73 (international code: 1)

Founded in 1885, Bank Line is one of the operating divisions of Andrew Weir Shipping. Its ships have sailed in the South Pacific for the past 80 years.

In 1990 the company decided to refurbish three of its cargo ships so that they could accommodate 9 passengers each. The success of this round-the-world trip via the South Pacific is such that a fourth cargo ship has been converted for passenger use.

The facilities on board are first-class. The passenger areas are spacious and elegant, each cabin has a radio, a video recorder for film viewing, and even tea and coffee-making facilities.

This voyage by cargo ship is one of the most appealing of all, as it calls at many South Pacific islands which are difficult to gain access to: Polynesia, Samoa, Fiji, New Caledonia, Vanuatu, the Salomon Islands and Papua New Guinea. Furthermore, as much of the cargo is conventional, the stopovers vary from one to four days.

This round-the-world voyage is often booked up a long time ahead during the popular winter season. The low season is between June and August. It is usually sold as a round trip, but if you only wish to do one part of it, you can ask to be put on a waiting list and hopefully receive confirmation six weeks before departure that a cabin is free. You could, for example, just take the Papeete–Singapore leg, a unique journey through the small islands of the South Pacific.

In 1994 Bank Line launched a new line for passengers on board the **Olivebank**: an unusual voyage which leaves the southeast USA and goes to South Africa and then Brazil before returning to Savannah. Calls at Tenerife or Abidjan are sometimes included.

Please note that these cargo ships do not look like giant container ships at all: their gracious elegance will delight nostalgic travellers.

Nationalities: British and Polish officers, Bangladeshi and Polish crew

Conditions: maximum age 82

Itinerary

Round trip: 110/130 days

129 ▼ Hamburg *Germany*
Hull *United Kingdom*
Antwerp *Belgium*
Dunkirk *France*
Le Havre *France*
Panama Canal
Papeete *Tahiti*
possibly: Apia *Samoa*
Suva *Fiji*
Lautoka *Fiji*
Noumea *New Caledonia*
Port Vila *Vanuatu*
Santo *Vanuatu*

Honiara *Solomon Islands*
Yandina *Solomon Islands*
Lae *Papua New Guinea*
Madang *Papua New Guinea*
Kimbe *Papua New Guinea*
Rabaul *Papua New Guinea*
Darwin *Australia*
Singapore
Suez Canal
Antwerp *Belgium*
Rotterdam *Holland*
Hamburg *Germany*
Hull *United Kingdom*

Ships and Fares

Clydebank, Ivybank, Forthbank, Moraybank:

Multi-purpose ships built in 1973/74, 15460 tons, modified to carry passengers in 1989/90, 9 passengers

Facilities: cabins with shower/wc, video, radio, refrigerator, salon, bar, veranda, pool

Round trip: $11,825 / $13,575 (Aug–Oct), or $95 to $110 per day.
Possible discounts in low season: June–Aug
Special prices for trips between 2 stopovers

Hull	▶	Papeete	26 days
Hull	▶	Noumea	39 days
Papeete	▶	Singapore	48 days
Noumea	▶	Hull	64 days

Itinerary

Round trip: about 75 days

153 ▼ Savannah *Georgia USA*   Cape Town *South Africa*
Newport News *Virginia USA*   Recife *Brazil*
Baltimore *Maryland USA*   La Guaira *Venezuela*
Canary Islands   San Juan *Puerto Rico*
Dakar *Senegal*   Veracruz *Mexico*
Abidjan *Ivory Coast*   Houston Texas *USA*
Cape Town *South Africa*   New Orleans *Louisiana USA*
Durban *South Africa*   Savannah *Georgia USA*

Several of the above ports are only occasional stopovers

Ships and Fares

Olivebank

28,080 tons, 8 passengers
Round trip: $7700/$8450, or $102 to $112 per day

Blue Star Line

Albion House
20 Queen Elizabeth Street
London SE1 2LS United Kingdom
✆ (0171) 407 2345, 🖷 (0171) 407 4636 (international code: 44)

Agent in USA:

> One World Trade Center, Suite 8101
> New York, N.Y. 10048 USA
> ✆ (212) 775 1500, 🖷 (212) 938 0516 (international code: 1)

In Great Britain in 1907 the Vestey brothers founded a company of refrigerated warehouses. By 1909 they needed to buy two refrigerated vessels in order to transport meat from South America. Little by little the number of ships grew, and even included five pre-war liners. They sailed to South Africa as well as Australasia and North America.

Today Blue Star Line has a large fleet of container ships and of vessels specialized in transporting fresh produce around the world. It is also associated to other members of the Vestey group. Since the merger between Blue Star and ACT/PACE in 1992 and since the purchase of new ships like the **Columbia Star**, it is now one of the largest companies to carry passengers to the South Pacific.

> **Nationalities:** British officers and crew
>
> **Conditions**: maximum age 80; medical certificate required over 70 years; luggage carried free (up to 4 suitcases per person)

Itinerary

Round trip: 49 days

29 ▼

Tilbury *United Kingdom*	Itajai *Brazil*
Hamburg *Germany*	Santos *Brazil*
Bremen *Germany*	Rio de Janeiro *Brazil*
Antwerp *Belgium*	Salvador *Brazil*
Recife/Suape *Brazil*	Le Havre *France*
Santos *Brazil*	Rotterdam *Holland*
Rio Grande *Brazil*	Tilbury *United Kingdom*

Itinerary may vary to include other ports: Buenos Aires *Argentina* and Lisbon *Portugal*.

Frequency: every seven weeks

NB: On this voyage, the vessel stops twice at some ports during the journey. It is therefore possible to stop over at some destinations and rejoin the voyage on the vessel's return.

Passengers who wish to stay in South America for several weeks may do so and rejoin the next voyage.

Ship and Fares

Argentina Star

22,635 tons, 12 passengers, 5 double cabins, 2 single cabins

Facilities: salon, bar, laundry room, gym, small pool

Round trip: £3010

Antwerp	▶	Recife	£ 860
In the other direction:			£1300
Antwerp	▶	Buenos Aires	£1175
Antwerp	▶	Salvador	£2000
Tilbury	▶	Recife	£1190
In the other direction:			£1215
Recife	▶	Rotterdam	£ 975

Itinerary   Round trip: 65–70 days

144 ▼ Jacksonville *Florida USA*
    or from one of the following east
    coast ports:
    Philadelphia, Norfolk, *or* Houston
    Panama
    Melbourne *Australia*
    Sydney *Australia*

Brisbane *Australia*
possibly:
Port Chalmers *New Zealand*
Wellington *New Zealand*
Auckland *New Zealand*
Panama
Philadelphia *Pennsylvania USA*

(One way: 20/35 days)

Fares

Round trip: $4760 (in low season)/$6800, or $70 to $120 per day
East coast USA to one port in either Australia or New Zealand:
$2650/$3550, or $90 to $140 per day

Itinerary   Round trip: 42–45 days

146 ▼ Los Angeles *California USA*
    Auckland *New Zealand*
    Sydney *Australia*
    Melbourne *Australia*
    Wellington *New Zealand*

Auckland *New Zealand*
Suva *Fiji*
Seattle *Washington USA*
Los Angeles *California USA*

Ships and Fares

Columbia Star and California Star

Round trip: $4400/$5300, or $97 to $117 per day

Los Angeles ▶	New Zealand	14 days	$1600/$2000
Los Angeles ▶	Australia	18 days	$2050/$2450

Columbus Line

Agent in UK:

The Strand Cruise and Travel Centre
Charing Cross Shopping Concourse
The Strand
London WC2N 4HZ United Kingdom
✆ (0171) 836 6363, ✉ (0171) 497 0078 (international code: 44)

Agent in Germany:

Hamburg-Süd Reiseagentur
Ost-West Str. 59–61
20457 Hamburg Germany
✆ (040) 37 05 155, ✉ (040) 37 05 24 20 (international code: 49)

Agent in USA:

Freighter World Cruise Inc.,
180 South Lake Avenue, Suite 335
Pasadena
California 91101 USA
✆ (818) 449 31 06, ✉ (818) 449 95 73 (international code: 1)

Despite its American-sounding name, this company, founded in 1871, is a subsidiary of the large Germany group, Hamburg-Süd. You can travel on its eight comfortable container ships from the USA to the South Pacific.

Conditions: maximum age 79

Ships

Columbus Virginia, Columbus Wellington
14,173 tons, 8 passengers

Oregon Star
8 passengers, 4 double cabins

Itinerary

Round trip: about 68 days

145 ▼ Jacksonville *Florida USA*
Houston *Texas USA*
Panama Canal
possibly: Auckland *New Zealand*
Melbourne *Australia*
Sydney *Australia*
possibly: Brisbane *Australia*

possibly:
Port Chalmers *New Zealand*
Wellington *New Zealand*
Auckland *New Zealand*
Panama Canal
possibly: Kingston *Jamaica*
Philadelphia *Pennsylvania USA*

Frequency: 1 or 2 sailings per month

Fares

Round trip:
$5450/$6070 March–Sept, or $80 to $90 per day
$7650/$8700 Oct–Feb, or $112 to $130 per day

Itinerary

Round trip: 42–45 days

147 ▼ Los Angeles *California USA*
Auckland *New Zealand*
Sydney *Australia*
Melbourne *Australia*
Wellington *New Zealand*

Auckland *New Zealand*
occasionally: Honolulu *Hawaii*
Seattle *Washington USA*
Los Angeles *California USA*

Frequency: 1 or 2 sailings per month

Fares

Round trip:
$4798/$7100 March–Sept, or $105 to $160 per day
$5400/$7370 Oct–Feb, or $120 to $165 per day

Compagnie Générale Maritime (C.G.M.)

C.G.M.
22 quai Galliéni
92158 Suresnes Cedex France
✆ 46 25 70 00, 🖷 46 25 78 00 (international code: 33)

Agents in France:

Mer et Voyages
3 rue Tronchet
75008 Paris France
✆ (1) 44 51 01 68, 📠 (1) 40 07 12 72 (international code: 33)

For the France–West Indies route:

Sotramat Voyages
12 rue Godot de Mauroy
75009 Paris France
✆ 49 24 24 73, 📠 47 42 04 53 (international code: 33)

For the West Indies Inter-island Route:

Transat Antilles Voyage
Quai Lefèvre Boîte Postale
Pointe-à-Pitre
Guadeloupe 97153
✆ 83 04 43/82 95 74 (international code: 590)

In response to demands from passengers, C.G.M. has gradually begun to open up new routes for its cargo ships.

Up until 1994, the famous banana boats (now container ships) linking France with the West Indies were the last C.G.M. ships to accept passengers on board. Since 1995 new itineraries are being looked into: towards the Orient as well as to South America, or round the world.

Note that C.G.M.'s Germany subsidiary, Horn Linie, also carries passengers to the Caribbean on its fruit carriers.

Nationalities: French officers and crew

Conditions: maximum age 80, minimum age 5
For passengers over 65, a medical certificate is required
Animals accepted under certain conditions
Cars and motorcycles accepted
Weight restriction on baggage: 150kg

Itinerary

Each way: 10/12 days

21 ▼   Le Havre *France*   *or* Pointe-à-Pitre *Guadeloupe*
         Fort-de-France *Martinique*   Le Havre *France*

Frequency: weekly

Ships and Fares

Fort Desaix, Fort Saint-Charles

Built in 1980, 28,955 tons, 12 passengers, 4 twin cabins, 4 single cabins

Fort Royal, Fort Fleur d'Epée

Built in 1979/80, 30,998 tons, 12 passengers, 4 twin cabins, 4 single cabins

Round trip:11,300F (low season); 12,550F (high season)

Le Havre ▶ 1st island port   5060F (Jan–June)
or: 5600F (July–Dec)
Le Havre ▶ 2nd island port   5700F (Jan–June)
or: 6300F (July–Dec)

Single cabin supplement: 400F

| 1st island port | ▶ | Le Havre | 5600F or: 6310F |
| 2nd island port | ▶ | Le Havre | 5060F or: 5700F |

30% discount for children aged 5–12
20% discount for young people aged 12–27

Itinerary

Round trip: about 56 days

95 ▼   Le Havre *France*
Port Said *Egypt*
Port Kelang *Malaysia*
Singapore
Hong Kong
Pusan *North Korea*
Kobe *Japan*

Shimizu *Japan*
Nagoya *Japan*
Yokohama *Japan*
Hong Kong (*second call*)
Singapore (*second call*)
Suez Canal
Le Havre *France*

(Route under consideration; for further details contact the Mer et Voyages agency)

Ships and Fares

CGM Normandie

Round trip: 27,500F, or 500F per day

Le Havre	▶	Port Kelang	17 days
Le Havre	▶	Singapore	18 days
Le Havre	▶	Hong Kong	22 days
Le Havre	▶	Pusan	25 days
Le Havre	▶	Kobe	27 days
Hong Kong	▶	Le Havre	21 days
Singapore	▶	Le Havre	18 days

Itinerary   Round trip: about 56 days

96 ▼

La Spezia *Italy*	Kobe *Japan*
Barcelona *Spain*	Nagoya *Japan*
Fos-sur-mer *France*	Yokohama *Japan*
Damietta *Egypt*	Hong Kong (*second call*)
Port Said *Egypt*	Singapore (*second call*)
possibly: Jeddah *Saudi Arabia*	Port Kelang *Malaysia*
Singapore	Suez Canal
Hong Kong	Damietta *Egypt*
Pusan *South Korea*	La Spezia *Italy*

(Route under consideration, for further details contact the Mer et Voyages agency)

Ships and Fares

CGM Pasteur, CGM Pascal

Round trip: 28,000F, or 500F per day

Fos-sur-mer	▶	Damietta	4 days
Fos-sur-mer	▶	Singapore	17 days
Fos-sur-mer	▶	Hong Kong	21 days
Fos-sur-mer	▶	Pusan	24 days
Fos-sur-mer	▶	Kobe	26 days
Hong Kong	▶	La Spezia	20 days
Singapore	▶	La Spezia	16 days

Itinerary

Round trip: about 77 days

130 ▼ Le Havre *France*
Savannah *Georgia USA*
Cristobal *Panama*
Papeete *Tahiti*
possibly: Don Iambo *Mururoa*
Noumea *New Caledonia*
Melbourne *Australia*
Sydney *Australia*

Brisbane *Australia*
Lae *Papua New Guinea*
Jakarta *Indonesia*
Colombo *Sri Lanka*
Suez Canal
Genoa *Italy*
Marseilles *France*

(Route not yet in operation)

Ships and Fares

CGM Rimbaud, CGM Renoir, CGM Ronsard, CGM Racine

Round trip: 38,500F, or 500F per day

Itinerary

Round trip: 1 week

141 ▼ *Inter-island voyages between*
Martinique and Puerto Rico:
Pointe-à-Pitre *Martinique*
St Kitts (*1 call in 3*)
Antigua/St Barthélémy/St Martin

San Juan *Puerto Rico*
St Martin
Montserrat
Pointe-à-Pitre *Martinique*

Rotation:

Sat: Pointe-à-Pitre. Sun: St Kitts (1 call in 3). Mon: Antigua/St Barth/ St Martin. Tues: San Juan. Wed: San Juan. Thurs: St Martin. Fri: Montserrat. Sat: Pointe-à-Pitre.

Ships and Fares

Sunshine Pearl

2 single cabins, 1 double cabin
Fare per day: $80

Compagnie Maritime Française de Tahiti

B.P. 368, Papeete
Tahiti, French Polynesia

For the cargo ship **Temehani**:
S.A. Navigation Temehani
B.P. 9015, Papeete
Tahiti, French Polynesia

Two cargo ships from different shipping companies maintain a regular service
between the islands around Tahiti: the **Taporo** of the Compagnie Maritime
Française de Tahiti, and the **Temehani** of the company of the same name.

Itinerary

Round trip: 4 days

170 ▼ *Inter-island voyages between*   Bora Bora
Tahiti and Bora Bora: Papeete
Papeete *Tahiti*   Bora Bora
Various neighbouring islands in   Tahaa
French Polynesia: Raiatea
Huahine   Huahine
Raiatea   Papeete
Tahaa

Fares: on demand
Passengers may travel either on deck or in a cabin

Compagnie Polynésienne de Transport Maritime

B.P. 220, Papeete
Tahiti, French Polynesia
✆ 42 62 40/43, 🖷 43 48 89 (international code: 689)

Agent in UK:

The Strand Cruise and Travel Centre
Charing Cross Shopping Concourse
The Strand
London WC2N 4HZ United Kingdom
✆ (0171) 836 6363, 🖷 (0171) 497 0078 (international code: 44)

Agent in France:

Le Quotidien Voyages
119 av. Charles de Gaulle
92200 Neuilly France
✆ 47 47 11 16, 🖷 46 24 34 88

Agent in USA:

> Freighter World Cruise Inc.,
> 180 South Lake Avenue, Suite 335
> Pasadena
> California 91101 USA
> ✆ (818) 449 31 06, ✉ (818) 449 95 73 (international code: 1)

A real passenger-cargo ship, 103m long, the **Aranui** ('Great Path' in Maori) sails between Tahiti and the Marquesas Islands—the last descendant of the schooners which carried copra and travellers around the islands. The ship is manned by 32 Polynesian sailors.

The **Aranui** links the Marquesas islands and the Tuamotu islands to the rest of the world and carries about a hundred passengers, mainly inhabitants of the islands. Some travel on the decks; there are about 30 cabins for those who wish to travel more comfortably.

This relaxing 16-day voyage through the most beautiful islands of Polynesia is without doubt one of the most spectacular you could ever wish for. It has been enthusiastically written about in newspapers and on television in the USA. One journalist called the trip 'anti-cruise'.

The **Aranui** allows you to visit islands which otherwise would be difficult to reach. You often need to use dugout canoes to go ashore.

> **Nationalities:** French Polynesian officers and crew
>
> **Conditions:** no age limit

Itinerary

Round trip: 15 days

171 ▼ *Inter-island voyages between Tahiti and the Marquesas Islands*:
Papeete *Tahiti*
Takapoto *Tuamotou*

Ua Pou, Nuku Hiva, Hiva Oa, Fatu Hiva, Hiva Oa, Ua Huka, Nuku Hiva *Marquesas Islands*
Rangiroa *Tuamotou*
Papeete *Tahiti*

Ships and Fares

Aranui

> (Formerly named the Bremer Horst Biscoff), built in 1989, 4200 tons, 60 passengers

Facilities: video lounge, library, pool, activities available include excursions, fishing and diving

Round trip: Rear deck (mattress and sheets provided, toilets on the deck): 8415F, or 495F per day

Inside cabins: 15,427F

Deluxe accommodation: 21,144F

Children between the ages of 3 and 15 sharing a cabin with their parents: 4400F

Discounts are available (15%) for passengers over 60 years and also at certain times of year)

For single cabins, there is a surcharge of 50%

Containerschiffs Reederei

Agent in Germany:

Hamburg-Süd Reiseagentur
Ost-West Str. 59–61
20457 Hamburg Germany
✆ (040) 37 05 155, ✆ (040) 37 05 24 20 (international code: 49)

Agent in UK:

The Strand Cruise and Travel Centre
Charing Cross Shopping Concourse
The Strand
London WC2N 4HZ United Kingdom
✆ (0171) 836 6363, ✆ (0171) 497 0078 (international code: 44)

Agent in USA:

Freighter World Cruise Inc.,
180 South Lake Avenue, Suite 335
Pasadena
California 91101 USA
✆ (818) 449 31 06 ✆ (818) 449 95 73 (international code: 1)

Ship

Alum Bay

21600 tons, 6 passengers

Itinerary

Round trip: about 28 days

3 ▼   Genoa *Italy*
       Valencia *Spain*
       Cadiz *Spain*
       Lisbon *Portugal*

Montreal *Canada*
Salerno *Italy*
Livorno *Italy*
Genoa *Italy*

Fares

Round trip: $2436/$2800 $, or $87 to $100 per day

Itinerary

Round trip: about 28 days

44 ▼   Rotterdam *Holland*
        Algeciras *Spain*
        Piraeus *Greece*
        Izmir *Turkey*
        Salonika *Greece*

Piraeus *Greece*
Algeciras *Spain*
Felixstowe *United Kingdom*
Rotterdam *Holland*

Fares

Round trip: DM3920/DM4480, or DM140/DM160 per day

Deutsche Seereederei Rostock

Agents in Germany:

Frachtschiff-Touristik (Captain Peter Zylmann)
Exhöft 12
24404 Maasholm Germany
℡ 0 4642 60 68, 🖷 0 4642 67 67 (international code: 49)

Hamburg-Süd Reiseagentur

Ost-West Str. 59–61
20457 Hamburg Germany
✆ (040) 37 05 155, ✇ (040) 37 05 24 20 (international code: 49)

Agent in UK:

The Strand Cruise and Travel Centre
Charing Cross Shopping Concourse
The Strand
London WC2N 4HZ United Kingdom
✆ (0171) 836 6363, ✇ (0171) 497 0078 (international code: 44)

In USA:

Freighter World Cruise Inc.
180 South Lake Avenue, Suite 335
Pasadena
California 91101 USA
✆ (818) 449 31 06, ✇ (818) 449 95 73 (international code: 1)

Deutsche Seereederei Rostock was East Germany's national shipping company and has recently been restructured. It has now changed hands and has teamed up with Senator Line, namely for the round-the-world route.

You can travel on numerous routes to the Far East, Latin America, Canada or Africa on its cargo ships, container ships or bulk carriers.

Ships

DSR Baltic, DSR Atlantic, DSR Pacific, DSR Europe, DSR Asia, DSR America

6 sister container ships, built in 1992; 4 passengers

Itinerary   Round trip: about 35 days

4 ▼   Livorno/Genoa *Italy*   Izmir *Turkey*
       Valencia *Spain*   Naples *Italy*
       Montreal *Canada*   Genoa/Livorno *Italy*
       Larnaka *Cyprus*

       Frequency: monthly sailings

Fare

Round trip: DM4225, or DM120 per day

Genoa/Livorno	▶ Montreal	about 13 days	DM1695
Valencia	▶ Montreal	about 11 days	DM1465
Montreal	▶ Larnaka	about 13 days	DM1695
Montreal	▶ Naples	about 21 days	DM2730

Itinerary

Round trip: about 7/8 weeks

18 ▼   Hamburg *Germany*   Rio Haina *Dominican Republic*
San Juan *Puerto Rico*   San Juan *Puerto Rico*
Veracruz *Mexico*   Antwerp *Belgium*
Tampico *Mexico*   Hamburg *Germany*
possibly: La Guaira *Venezuela*

Fares

Round trip: DM6060/DM7518, or DM108 to DM134 per day

Hamburg	▶ San Juan	about 13 days	DM1550/DM1900
Hamburg	▶ Veracruz	about 20 days	DM2320/DM2860
Veracruz	▶ Hamburg	about 34 days	DM3860/DM4778
San Juan	▶ Hamburg	about 16 days	DM1880/DM2312

Dobson Lines

Agent in UK:

The Strand Cruise and Travel Centre
Charing Cross Shopping Concourse
The Strand
London WC2N 4HZ United Kingdom
✆ (0171) 836 6363, ✉ (0171) 497 0078 (international code: 44)

The history of this British company goes back to 1966 when S.G. Dobson Ltd, a private family company, was founded by Mr S.G. Dobson. Over the years the company has gone from strength to strength and in 1993 Dobson Fleet Management Limited (DFM) was established.

Now based in Cyprus, the company owns five bulk carriers, two of which have been refurbished and refitted to carry a small group of passengers. They are very traditional vessels with excellent deck space and, because they are bulk carriers, they carry no containers and have unrestricted views.

The vessels operate interesting itineraries which can vary for every voyage and therefore it is necessary for passengers to be very flexible with their dates before making a reservation. **Jenny D** and **Karen D** will start carrying passengers from autumn 1995. Fares have yet to be confirmed at the time of writing, but should be approximately £50–£55 per day.

Ships

Jenny D

Built 1972, 11,625 tons. Sails to Europe, Atlantic and the Caribbean

Karen D

Built 1970, 5306 tons. Sails to Europe and the Caribbean

Facilities: both vessels have comfortable accommodation for 4/5 passengers each. There is an outdoor swimming pool, a small lounge/library with TV/video.

Dollart Reederei

Agent in Germany:

Hamburg-Süd Reiseagentur
Ost-West Str. 59–61
20457 Hamburg Germany
✆ (040) 37 05 155, ✇ (040) 37 05 24 20 (international code: 49)

Agent in UK:

The Strand Cruise and Travel Centre
Charing Cross Shopping Concourse
The Strand
London WC2N 4HZ United Kingdom
✆ (0171) 836 6363, ✇ (0171) 497 0078 (international code: 44)

Agent in USA:

Freighter World Cruise Inc.
180 South Lake Avenue, Suite 335
Pasadena
California 91101 USA
✆ (818) 449 31 06, ✇ (818) 449 95 73 (international code: 1)

A German shipping company whose vessels, the **Calapadria** and the **CGM Iguaçu** (built in 1984), sail from the Mediterranean to Brazil.

Itinerary

Round trip: about 50 days

28 ▼   Genoa *Italy*
Fos-sur-mer *France*
Barcelona *Spain*
Fortaleza *Brazil*
Salvador *Brazil*
Santos *Brazil*
Buenos Aires *Argentina*
Montevideo *Uruguay*
Sao Francisco do Sul *Brazil*

Vitoria *Brazil*
Salvador *Brazil*
Tenerife *Canary Islands*
Las Palmas *Canary Islands*
Valencia *Spain*
Livorno *Italy*
Naples *Italy*
Genoa *Italy*

Fares

Round trip: DM6500/DM8750, or DM130 to DM175 per day

Genoa	▶	Vitoria	about 16 days	DM2080/DM2800
Genoa	▶	Buenos Aires	about 22 days	DM2860/DM3850
Buenos Aires	▶	Canary Islands	about 20 days	DM2600/DM3500
Buenos Aires	▶	Genoa	about 28 days	DM3640/DM4900
Santos	▶	Valencia	about 17 days	DM2210/DM2975

Egon Oldendorff

PO Box 2135
Funfhausen 1
D-2400 Lübeck 1 Germany
✆ (0451) 15 00 0, ✉ (0451) 7 35 22 (international code: 49)

Agents in UK:

The Cruise People Ltd
106 Seymour Place
London W1H 5DG
✆ (0171) 723 2450 (international code: 44)

The Strand Cruise and Travel Centre
Charing Cross Shopping Concourse
The Strand
London WC2N 4HZ United Kingdom
✆ (0171) 836 6363, ✉ (0171) 497 0078 (international code: 44)

Agent in France:

> Mer et Voyages
> 3 rue Tronchet
> 75008 Paris France
> ✆ (1) 44 51 01 68, ✉ (1) 40 07 12 72 (international code: 33)

Agent in USA:

> Norton Lilly & Co., Operations Department
> 245 Monticello Arcade
> Norfolk VA 23510 USA
> ✆ (804) 622 70 35, ✉ (804) 622 47 59 (international code: 1)

Agent in Canada:

> Egon Marine Services,
> 9240 Patterson Road,
> Richmond, BC, V6X 1P7 Canada
> ✆ (604) 671 54 61, ✉ (604) 273 56 41 (international code: 1)

Agent in Australia:

> Sydney International Travel Center Pty. Ltd,
> Reid House, 75 King Street, 8th floor,
> Sydney NSW 2000 Australia
> ✆ (2) 299 80 00, ✉ (2) 299 13 37 (international code: 61)

Those who love travelling by cargo ship will be bound to recognize the name of Egon Oldendorff, one of the most well-known lines. With this company you can travel at competitive prices to almost any destination you care to name.

Its fleet consists of about 30 boats: bulk carriers of 28,000 to 74,000 tons, as well as container ships of 15,000 to 23,000 tons. Most have air-conditioning and a small swimming pool.

This company practises 'tramp-shipping', which means that the routes of its cargo ships depend strictly on supply and demand. All you need to know is that it has offices all over the American continent, from Chile to Canada, in Africa, Indonesia, China or Japan, which just proves that its ships sail around the world on ever-changing itineraries. However, there are also more regular routes, like the transatlantic link between Europe and the USA and Canada, on board bulk carriers.

The list of itineraries below is therefore only provisional. It indicates a route followed by a ship at a particular time; it also gives an idea of the fares.

Ask for the most recent 'position list' to find out where the cargo ships are and what their destinations are. To quote an example, the summer 1994 position list showed vessels on their way to the USA, Brazil, Indonesia, the Far East, China, Japan, Chile, Argentina and South Africa.

Conditions: maximum age 75
Medical certificate required for travellers between 70 and 75
Children aged 1 to 12 years: 50% discount
Special fares for children under 1

Itinerary

One way: 10 to 12 days

1 ▼ A western European port (*often*: Ghent *Belgium*, Rotterdam *Holland*, Le Havre *France*, Hamburg *Germany*)
Sept-Iles/Port-Cartier/Baie-Comeau *Canada*

Montreal/Quebec *Canada*
occasionally: ports on the Great Lakes
Quebec *Canada*
A western European port

The ports on the Saint Lawrence river are only accessible from early May, due to ice.

Fares

Travelling from Europe to Canada:
Double cabin (per pers.): DM1000. Single cabin: DM1200
Or between DM83 and DM100 per day

Travelling from Canada to Europe:
Double cabin (per pers.): CAN $700. Single cabin: CAN $830

NB: 'Open' tickets may be bought, whereby the return portion of the ticket is valid for one year. If the return journey has not been made within that time, the cost of the return journey will be refunded on receipt of the ticket.

Itineraries

Round trip: about 42 days

7 ▼ Antwerp *Belgium*
Rotterdam *Holland*
Bremen *Germany*
Felixstowe *United Kingdom*
Wilmington *North Carolina USA*
Charleston *South Carolina USA*
Miami *Florida USA*
New Orleans *Louisiana USA*

Houston *Texas*
Charleston *South Carolina USA*
Wilmington *North Carolina USA*
Antwerp *Belgium*
Bremen *Germany*
Felixstowe *United Kingdom*
Le Havre *France*

19 ▼ Antwerp *Belgium*
Bremen *Germany*
Felixstowe *United Kingdom*
Le Havre *France*
Boston *Massachusetts USA*
Charleston *South Carolina USA*
Miami *Florida USA*
Veracruz *Mexico*
Altamira *Mexico*

Galveston *Texas USA*
Houston *Texas USA*
New Orleans *Louisiana USA*
Charleston *South Carolina USA*
Boston *Massachusetts USA*
Antwerp *Belgium*
Bremen *Germany*
Felixstowe *United Kingdom*
Le Havre *France*

Ships and Fares

Mixteco and **Maya**

Built in 1985
Round trip: DM4620/DM5460, or DM100/DM130 per day

Itinerary

One way: 10–12 days

10 ▼ A western European port (*often*:
Ghent *Belgium*, Rotterdam
Holland, Le Havre *France*,
Hamburg *Germany*)
Norfolk/Newport News *Virginia
USA*

occasionally:
Baltimore *Maryland*
Philadelphia *Pennsylvania*
Newark *New York*
Boston *Massachusetts USA*
A western European port

Fares

From the last European port to the first American port:
DM1200/DM1000

Egon Oldendorff   137

NB: 'Open' tickets may be bought, whereby the return portion of the ticket is valid for one year. If the return journey has not been made within that time, the cost of the return journey will be refunded on receipt of the ticket.

Itinerary

One way: about 14 days

12 ▼   A western European port (*often*:
         Ghent *Belgium*, Rotterdam
         Holland, Le Havre *France*,
         Hamburg *Germany*)
       Ports in southeastern USA:

New Orleans *Louisiana*,
Mobile *Alabama*, Houston
Texas, Galveston *Texas*,
Corpus Christi *Texas*
A western European port

Fares

From the last European port to the first American port:
DM1200/DM1400

Itinerary

Round trip: about 45 days

137 ▼ New York *USA*
       Philadelphia *Pennsylvania USA*
       Baltimore *Maryland USA*
       Norfolk *Virginia USA*
       Jacksonville *Florida USA*
       Miami *Florida USA*
       Fort-de-France *Martinique*
       Bridgetown *Barbados*
       Port of Spain *Trinidad*
       Rio de Janeiro *Brazil*
       Santos *Brazil*

Buenos Aires *Argentina*
Montevideo *Uruguay*
Imbituba *Brazil*
Itajai *Brazil*
Sao Francisco do Sul *Brazil*
Santos *Brazil*
Rio de Janeiro *Brazil*
Salvador *Brazil*
Recife *Brazil*
Fortaleza *Brazil*
New York *USA*

Ship and Fares

Columbus Olivos

Container ships built in 1980, 8 passengers
         Round trip: $4400/$4900, or $100 to $110 per day

Itinerary

Round trip: about 41 days

149 ▼ Vancouver *BC Canada*
Seattle *Washington USA*
Tomakomai *Japan*
Pusan *South Korea*
Kobe *Japan*

Nagoya *Japan*
Shimizu *Japan*
Tokyo *Japan*
Seattle *Washington USA*
Vancouver *BC Canada*

Fares

Round trip: DM4100/DM3690, or DM90/DM125 per day

Itinerary

Round trip: about 3 months

150 ▼ Esmeraldas *Ecuador*
Arica *Chile*
Iquique *Chile*
Valparaiso *Chile*
Chonoral *Chile*
Antofagasta *Chile*
Ilo *Peru*
Callao *Peru*
Yokohama *Japan*
Onahama *Japan*

Nagoya *Japan*
Kobe *Japan*
Pusan *South Korea*
Keelung *Taiwan*
Hong Kong
Pusan *South Korea*
Hiroshima *Japan*
Kobe *Japan*
Esmeraldas *Ecuador*

Ship and Fares

CCNI Austral

Container ship built in 1992
Fare per day: DM100/DM120

Itinerary

Round trip: about 6 weeks

160 ▼ Singapore
Jebel Ali *United Arab Emirates*
Dammam *United Arab Emirates*
Singapore
Yokohama *Japan*

Kobe *Japan*
Pusan *South Korea*
Keelung *Taiwan*
Shekou *Hong Kong*
Singapore

Fares

DM140/DM150 per day

Itinerary

Round trip: about 60 days

165 ▼ Hong Kong
    Keelung *Taiwan*
    Pusan *South Korea*
    Hiroshima *Japan*
    Osaka *Japan*
    Nagoya *Japan*
    Yokohama *Japan*
    Suva *Fiji or* Noumea
      New Caledonia

Auckland *New Zealand*
Napier *New Zealand*
Nelson *New Zealand*
Timaru *New Zealand*
Tauranga *New Zealand*
Suva *Fiji or* Noumea
  New Caledonia
Manila *Philippines*
Hong Kong

Fares

Round trip: DM7220/DM9280, or DM120 to DM155 per day

Itinerary

Round trip: about 56 days

166 ▼ Auckland *New Zealand*
    Lyttleton *New Zealand*
    Port Chalmers *New Zealand*
    Napier *New Zealand*
    Tauranga *New Zealand*
    Surabaya *Indonesia*
    Jakarta *Indonesia*

Port Kelang *Malaysia*
Singapore
Bangkok *Thailand*
Singapore
Noumea *New Caledonia*
Suva *Fiji*
Auckland *New Zealand*

Ship and Fares

NZOL Crusader

Container ship built in 1982

Round trip: DM6160/DM7280, or DM110 to DM130 per day

Itinerary

Round trip: about 30 days

167 ▼ Sydney *Australia*
    Melbourne *Australia*
    Brisbane *Australia*
    Yokohama *Japan*
    Osaka *Japan*

Pusan *South Korea*
Sydney *Australia*
Melbourne *Australia*
Brisbane *Australia*

Fares

Round trip: DM4200/DM4500, or DM140 to DM150 per day

Grimaldi

Agent in Italy:

Via Marchese Campodisola 13
80133 Naples Italy
☎ (081) 49 61 11, ✉ (081) 551 77 16 (international code: 39)

Agent in UK:

Associated Oceanic Agencies
103/105 Jermyn Street
London SW1Y 6ES United Kingdom
☎ (0171) 930 5683, ✉ (0171) 839 1986 (international code: 44)

Agent in France:

Transports et Voyages
32 rue du Quatre-Septembre
75002 Paris France
☎ 44 94 20 40, ✉ 42 66 15 80

At the end of the 1980s the Italian company Grimaldi surprised the maritime industry by putting into operation two giant ro-ro's able to transport new cars and about 60 passengers. It is one of the last companies to own passenger-cargo ships.

Its ships sail to West Africa, Brazil and the Mediterranean. On the 'Southern Cross Route', the atmosphere on board these car-carriers is similar to that on liners, with social activities, parties, ping-pong and card tournaments, language courses, and welcome and farewell ceremonies.

This company also has a liner, the **Ausonia**, which sails in the Mediterranean or the North Sea and holds conferences and conventions on board.

Nationalities: Italian officers and crew

Conditions: no age limit (doctor on board)

Ships

Repubblica de Venezia, Repubblica di Pisa

Built in 1987, 49,000 tons, 54 passengers
Facilities: lounge, bar, disco, video, gym, pool, sick bay

Repubblica di Genova, Repubblica di Amalfi

Built in 1989, 42,500 tons, 50 passengers
Facilities: lounge, disco, video, gym, pool, sick bay

Repubblica di Roma

Built in 1992, 40,000 tons, 12 passengers, 6 outside 2 berth cabins
Facilities: lounge, bar, TV/video room

Spes

Built in 1993, 33,400 tons, 12 passengers, 6 outside 2 berth cabins
with shower/wc

Fides

Built in 1993, 33,400 tons, 12 passengers, 6 outside 2 berth cabins
with shower/wc

Itinerary   Round trip: about 42 days

31 ▼   Tilbury *United Kingdom*   Vitoria *Brazil*
       Hamburg *Germany*   Santos *Brazil*
       Emden *Germany*   Paranagua *Brazil*
       Rotterdam *Holland*   Rio de Janeiro *Brazil*
       Antwerp *Belgium*   Tilbury *United Kingdom*
       Le Havre *France*

Fares

Round trip $2600/$5400
Europe   ▶   Brazil or Brazil   ▶   Europe: $1300–$3000

Itinerary   One way: 12/15 days

34 ▼   Genoa *Italy*   Salerno *Italy*
       Paranagua *Brazil*   Livorno *Italy*
       Santos *Brazil*   Genoa *Italy*
       Rio de Janeiro *Brazil*

       Frequency: fortnightly sailings

Fares

One way: $1100/$1400, or $91 to $116 per day

10% discount for return journeys, valid for 6 months
Children under 2 years of age free
Children from 2 to 12: 50% discount
Pets: $120
Cars: $900; caravans: $1300; motorcycles: $400

Itinerary

Round trip: about 1 month

42 ▼ Gothenburg *Sweden*
Antwerp *Belgium*
Southampton *United Kingdom*
Livorno *Italy*
Piraeus *Greece*

Limassol *Cyprus*
Ashdod *Israel*
Salerno/Savona *Italy*
A western European port

Frequency: monthly sailings

Fares

Northern Europe ▶ Italy/Spain (or vice-versa):
$850/$1250, cars: $360
Northern Europe ▶ Eastern Mediterranean (or vice-versa):
$1380/$2065, cars: $600
Italy ▶ Israel (or vice-versa):
$850/$1250, cars: $360

Round trip: 10% discount on return tickets; 'open' tickets must be used
within 6 months
Children under 12 years of age: 50% discount

Itinerary

Round trip: 35 days

63 ▼ Tilbury *United Kingdom*
Hamburg *Germany*
Amsterdam *Holland*
Antwerp *Belgium*
Le Havre *France*
Dakar *Senegal*
Conakry *Guinea*

Freetown *Sierra Leone*
Cotonou *Benin*
Lomé *Togo*
Tema *Ghana*
Lagos *Nigeria*
Douala *Cameroon*
Tilbury *United Kingdom*

Fares

Round trip: $2800–$4600

Europe ▶ Dakar/Conakry/Freetown:	$1250–$2100
Lomé/Cotonou/Lagos/Tema/Douala–Europe:	$1250–$2100
Europe to Lomé/Cotonou/Lagos/Tema/Douala:	$1600–$2700
Dakar/Conakry/Freetown ▶ Europe:	$1600–$2700

Horn Linie

Horn-Linie
Johannisbollwerk 6–8
D-20459 Hamburg Germany
✆ (040) 319 57 79, 🖷 (40) 319 40 40 (international code: 49)

Agent in France:

Mer et Voyages
3 rue Tronchet
75008 Paris France
✆ (1) 44 51 01 68, 🖷 (1) 40 07 12 72

Agent in UK:

The Strand Cruise Centre
Charing Cross Shopping Concourse
The Strand
London WC2N 4HZ United Kingdom
✆ (0171) 836 6363, 🖷 (0171) 497 0078 (international code: 44)

Founded in 1882, this shipping company based in Hamburg is a subsidiary of C.G.M. (Compagnie Générale Maritime). You can travel in luxurious conditions on its regular service to the Caribbean and Central America, on board its refrigerated cargo ships of the con-ro type (container ship and ro-ro).

Nationalities: German officers, international crew

Conditions: maximum age 75, minimum age 6

Itinerary

Round trip: about 35 days

22 ▼   Hamburg *Germany*   Moin *Costa Rica*
        Le Havre *France*   Dover *United Kingdom*
        Pointe-à-Pitre *Guadeloupe*   Antwerp *Belgium*
        Fort-de-France *Martinique*   Hamburg *Germany*
        St Lucia (*occasional calls*)

        Frequency: fortnightly sailings

Ships and Fares

Horncliff, Horncap, Hornbay

Built in Croatia in 1990, 1991, 1992, 12,887 tons, 12 passengers, 6 double cabins

Round trip: DM4990/DM5590, or DM142 to DM159 per day

Le Havre	▶	Caribbean/Costa Rica	DM2990/DM3290
Caribbean	▶	Le Havre	DM2990/DM3290
Costa Rica	▶	Le Havre	DM2390/DM2690

Weekly departures from Le Havre on Thursdays

5% rebate for passengers travelling for the second time with this company

Hurtigruten

Troms Fylkes Dampskibsselskap
A/S, PO Box 548
9001 Tromsø Norway
✆ (083) 86088, 🖷 (083) 88710 (international code: 47)

Agent in France:

Scanditours
140 rue du Faubourg Saint-Honoré
75008 Paris France
✆ (1) 45 61 74 50, 🖷 (1) 45 61 65 06 (international code: 33)

Agent in UK:

Norwegian State Railways
21/24 Cockspur Street
London SW1Y 5DA United Kingdom
℡ (0171) 930 6666, ✆ (0171) 321 0624 (international code: 44)

Three shipping companies (OVDS/TFDS/FFR) are grouped under the 'Hurtigruten' name. Their ships link the Norwegian ports of Bergen in the south and Kirkenes in the north, and stop at many small ports at the end of fjords, where large cruise liners are unable to go. In operation since 1893 as a postal service, this spectacular voyage has acquired an extraordinary reputation —to the point where there is one departure every day of the year from Bergen.

The 12 ships are very comfortable and, apart from the post, they carry cars and between 144 and 230 passengers. The stopovers last between a quarter of an hour and five hours.

Conditions: no age limit

Itinerary

Round trip: 12 days

103 ▼ *Voyage along the Norwegian coastline*:

Bergen
Florø
Måløy
Torvik
Ålesund
Molde
Kristiansund
Trondheim
Rorvik
Brønnøysund
Sandnessjøen
Nesna
Ørnes
Bodø
Lofoten Islands: Stamsund, Svolvaer, Stokmarknes, Sortland, Risoyhamn, Harstad

Finnsnes
Tromsø
Skjervoy
Oksfjord
Alta
Hammerfest
Havoysund
Honningsvag
Kjollefjord
Mehamn
Berlevag
Batsfjord
Vardo
Vadsø
Kirkenes
Bergen

Fares

Bergen ▶ Kirkenes (6 days)

1 June–31 Aug:	4980F/8820F	
Oct:	4020F/8820F	
1 Nov–28 Feb:	4900F/6680F	(only 3 to 4 hours of daylight per day)
Mar:	5370F/7420F	(the days are already longer than in Britain, and you can still appreciate the snow)

H. W. Janssen

Agent in Germany:

Hamburg-Süd Reiseagentur
Ost-West Str. 59–61
20457 Hamburg Germany
✆ (040) 37 05 155, ✇ (040) 37 05 24 20 (international code: 49)

Agent in UK:

The Strand Cruise and Travel Centre
Charing Cross Shopping Concourse
The Strand
London WC2N 4HZ United Kingdom
✆ (0171) 836 6363, ✇ (0171) 497 0078 (international code: 44)

This shipping company operates two routes between Great Britain and the Mediterranean on board the **City of London** and the **Sea Progress**.

Conditions: maximum age 79

Itinerary

Round trip: about 28 days

45 ▼ Felixstowe *United Kingdom*
Algeciras *Spain*
Piraeus *Greece*
Izmir *Turkey*
Salonika *Greece*

Piraeus *Greece*
Algeciras *Spain*
Rotterdam *Holland*
Felixstowe *United Kingdom*

(On another route there are stops in Cyprus and Israel; the return voyage calls at Belgium, Holland and Germany)

Fares

Round trip: £2100/£2360, or £75 to £84 per day

Felixstowe   ▶   Piraeus (1st stop)   £884 /£970

Icelandic Steamship (Eimskip)

Eimskip
Urval Travel
Alfabakka 16, PO Box 9180
Reykjavik 129 Iceland
✆ (91) 69 93 00, ✇ (91) 67 02 02 (international code: 354)

Agent in Germany:

Island Tours, Raboisen 5
20095 Hamburg Germany
✆ (040) 33 66 57, ✇ (040) 32 42 14 (international code: 49)

Agents in UK:

Arctic Experience Ltd
29 Nork Way
Banstead
Surrey CM7 1PB
✆ (01737) 362321 (international code: 44)

The Strand Cruise and Travel Centre
Charing Cross Shopping Concourse
The Strand
London WC2N 4HZ United Kingdom
✆ (0171) 836 6363, ✇ (0171) 497 0078 (international code: 44)

Since this Icelandic shipping company has begun to take passengers on board its cargo ships again, demand is such that you should book four to five months ahead for a cabin in the summer and one to two months ahead the rest of the time.

Conditions: no age limit

Itinerary

Round trip: 8 days

104 ▼ Immingham *United Kingdom*   Hamburg *Germany*
      Reykjavik *Iceland*   Rotterdam *Holland*
      Immingham *United Kingdom*   Immingham *United Kingdom*

Ships and Fares

Laxfoss, Bruarfoss

10,000 tons, 18 passengers, 6 cabins with 3 beds

Facilities: cabins with cable TV, video, radio, minibar, shower/wc; lounge, sauna, restaurant, pool, games room for children

Round trip: £502/£812, or £62 to £101 per day
(sailing from Immingham)

Immingham   ▶   Reykjavik   £251/£406

Same prices apply when travelling from Reykjavik–Immingham

Ivaran Lines

Vollsveien 9–11
PO Box 175, Lysaker
1324 Oslo Norway
✆ (02) 53 93 10, 📠 (02) 53 17 60 (international code: 47)

Agent in UK:

The Strand Cruise Centre
Charing Cross Shopping Concourse
The Strand
London WC2N 4HZ United Kingdom
✆ (0171) 836 6363, 📠 (0171) 497 0078 (international code: 44)

Agent in USA:

Ivaran Agencies, Newport Financial Center
111 Pavonia Avenue
Jersey City, NJ 0731–1755 USA
✆ (201) 798 56 56, 📠 (201) 798 22 33 (international code: 1)

This Norwegian company was founded in 1902 by Ivar Anton Christensen. Today it operates a route between New York and the east coast of South America. In 1988 it launched a cargo ship unlike any other: the **Americana**, one of today's rare passenger-cargo ships, a compromise between a cargo ship and a cruise liner.

The cabins are very elegant and spacious. It is undoubtedly the most luxurious (and the most expensive) passenger-cargo ship around at the moment, equipped to accommodate up to 80 passengers. Perhaps the first of a new generation?

A more conventional container vessel, the **San Antonio**, carrying 12 passengers, also operates to the east coast of South America. It is not fitted out quite as luxuriously as the **Americana** and is not as expensive.

Nationalities: Norwegian officers and crew

Conditions: no age limit (doctor on board)

Ships

Americana

Built in 1988, 19,203 tons, 80 passengers

Facilities: cabins with shower/wc, video, minibar, refrigerator, telephone, safe; lounge with dance floor, bar, casino, library, hairdresser, sauna/jacuzzi, pool, health club, sick bay, entertainment

San Antonio

Built in 1993, 20,000 tons, 12 passengers, 3 twin bedded cabins with shower/wc, 6 single cabins with shower/wc. Cabins fitted with TV, video and refrigerator. Lounge with TV/video, outdoor swimming pool.

Itinerary   Round trip: about 52 days

133 ▼ New Orleans *Louisiana USA*   Santos *Brazil*
      Houston *Texas USA*   Rio de Janeiro *Brazil*
      Puerto Cabello *Venezuela*   *possibly*: Salvador/Fortaleza
      La Guaira *Venezuela*   *Brazil*
      Rio de Janeiro *Brazil*   Bridgetown *Barbados*
      Santos *Brazil*   San Juan *Puerto Rico*
      Buenos Aires *Argentina*   Veracruz *Mexico*
      Montevideo *Uruguay*   Tampico *Mexico*
      Rio Grande *Brazil*   New Orleans *Louisiana USA*
      Itajai *Brazil*

Fares

Round trip in low season: $10,140/$14,820, or $195/$285 per day
Round trip in high season: $11,440/$17,160, or $220/$330 per day

Some single cabins can accommodate a second passenger in an upper couchette. In these circumstances the second passenger pays half price

Itinerary

Round trip: 44 days

135 ▼ Port Elizabeth *New Jersey USA*
Baltimore *Maryland USA*
Norfolk *Virginia USA*
Savannah *Georgia USA*
Miami *Florida USA*
Puerto Cabello *Venezuela*
La Guaira *Venezuela*
Rio de Janeiro *Brazil*
Santos *Brazil*

Buenos Aires *Argentina*
Montevideo *Uruguay*
Rio Grande *Brazil*
Itajai *Brazil*
Santos *Brazil*
Rio de Janeiro *Brazil*
possibly:
Salvadore/Fortaleza *Brazil*
Port Elizabeth *New Jersey USA*

Fares

Round trip: $5940–$7040, or $135–$160 per day

Jugolinija

P.O. Box 379
51000 Rijeka, Croatia

This Croatian company has operated various routes with its cargo ships for many years. During the 1970s and '80s you could still board at Dubrovnik and sail up the St Lawrence river to Montreal and beyond, to the ports of the Great Lakes.

Itinerary

One way: about 25/30 days

35 ▼ Rijeka *Croatia*
(*Different destinations depending on voyage*)

Buenos Aires *Argentina*
Rijeka *Croatia*

Fares: not supplied.

Leonhardt & Blumberg

Agents in Germany:

> Frachtschiff-Touristik (Captain Peter Zylmann)
> Exhöft 12
> 24404 Maasholm Germany
> ✆ 0 46 42 60 68, ✇ 0 46 42 67 67 (international code: 49)

> Hamburger Abendblatt–Die Welt
> Verkaufsburö/Seetouristik
> Große Bleichen 68
> 20354 Hamburg Germany
> ✆ (040) 347 2 49 17, ✇ (040) 35 27 96 (international code: 49)

Agent in UK:

> The Strand Cruise and Travel Centre
> Charing Cross Shopping Concourse
> The Strand
> London WC2N 4HZ United Kingdom
> ✆ (0171) 836 6363, ✇ (0171) 497 0078 (international code: 44)

Agent in Italy:

> L. Di Russo
> Via S. Maria
> Ponza Italy
> ✆ (0771) 80784 (international code: 39)

Agent in USA:

> Freighter World Cruises
> 180 South Lake Avenue, Suite 335
> Pasadena
> California 91101 USA
> ✆ (818) 449 31 06, ✇ (818) 449 95 73 (international code: 1)

In response to passengers' demands, you can now travel on numerous routes to the Far East with this German company, on cargo ships like the **Ville de Saturne** and the **Ville de Mars**, leaving from Europe as well as California.

Itinerary

Round trip: about 56 days

84 ▼   Bremen *Germany*   Hong Kong
       Southampton *United Kingdom*   Singapore
       Algeciras *Spain*   Colombo *Sri Lanka*
       Suez Canal   Suez Canal
       Jeddah *Saudi Arabia*   Algeciras *Spain*
       Jebel Ali/Dubai *United*   Rotterdam *Holland*
           Arab Emirates   Bremen *Germany*

Fares

Round trip: DM6954/DM10,753, or DM124 to DM192 per day

Algeciras ▶ Far East ▶ Algeciras	about 44 days	DM5505/DM8497
Bremen ▶ Hong Kong	about 29 days	DM3705/DM5677
Singapore ▶ Algeciras	about 17 days	DM2265/DM3421

Itinerary

Round trip: about 72 days

90 ▼   Hamburg *Germany*   Pusan *South Korea*
       Rotterdam *Holland*   Keelung (Chilung) *Taiwan*
       Antwerp *Belgium*   Kaohsiung *Taiwan*
       Isle of Grain *United Kingdom*   Hong Kong
       Le Havre *France*   Singapore
       Damietta *Egypt*   Colombo *Sri Lanka*
       Suez Canal   Suez Canal
       Jeddah *Saudi Arabia*   Damietta *Egypt*
       Fujairah *United Arab Emirates*   Fos-sur-mer *France*
       Singapore   Barcelona *Spain*
       Hong Kong   Hamburg *Germany*

Fares

Round trip: DM8865/DM13761, or DM123 to DM191 per day

| Hamburg ▶ Singapore | about 27 days | DM3465/DM5301 |

Same prices apply to travel from Singapore to Hamburg

| Hamburg ▶ Hong Kong | about 31 days | DM3945/DM6053 |

Itinerary

93 ▼ Hamburg *Germany*
Gothenburg *Sweden*
Hamburg *Germany*
Rotterdam *Holland*
Southampton *United Kingdom*
Port Said *Egypt*
Suez Canal
Singapore
Hong Kong
Pusan *South Korea*
Shimizu *Japan*

Yokohama *Japan*
Keelung (Chilung) *Taiwan*
Hong Kong
Singapore
Suez Canal
Southampton *United Kingdom*
Rotterdam *Holland*
Hamburg *Germany*
Gothenburg *Sweden*
Hamburg *Germany*

Fares

Round trip: DM7280/DM8400, or DM130 to DM150 per day

Lykes Lines

Lykes Cargoliner Passenger Service
Lykes Center, 300 Poydras Street
New Orleans
Louisiana 70130 USA
✆ (504) 523 66 11, ✉ (504) 528 12 71 (international code: 1)

Agent in Italy:

Lykes Lines, Piazza Corvetto 2–7
16122 Genoa, Italy
✆ 10 811 651, ✉ 10 873 566 (international code: 39)

This American company based in New Orleans has a large fleet of container ships, ro-ro's, and bulk carriers (transporting cereal, amongst other things), able to accommodate between four and 12 passengers each in luxurious conditions. The cabins are spacious and include a bath, shower and wc.

Because of changing itineraries and the large number of cargo ships owned by this company, it is best to contact them when you plan to leave in order to find out the up-to-date positions of the vessels. Lykes Lines ships are everywhere—in North and South America, Africa, the Mediterranean, Asia, the Far East—and offer numerous travel opportunities.

The Lykes company has begun a restructuring phase as they now receive no subsidy from the American government. Some of its vessels date from the 1960s and it has bought some more up-to-date cargo ships, notably from a company called Nedlloyd.

Conditions: maximum age 79

Itinerary

15 ▼   A port in southeastern *USA*   Tunisia, Egypt, Israel, Turkey
        A Mediterranean port *which*   Galveston *Texas USA*
          could include: Morocco, Italy,

(Round trip: between 30 and 50 days for bulk carriers, 30/32 days for container ships)

Frequency
Bulk carriers: monthly sailings
Container ships: sailings every 12–13 days

Fares

Round trip on bulk carriers: $3425/$5500, or $70 to $110 per day
Round trip on container ships: $3950, or $80 per day

Itinerary   One way: about 12 days

20 ▼   Felixstowe *United Kingdom*   Le Havre *France*
        Antwerp *Belgium*   New Orleans *Louisiana USA*
        Bremen *Germany*   Galveston *Texas USA*

Fares

Tickets for this voyage are usually sold as round-trip tickets, starting from the United States, but one-way tickets across the Atlantic can sometimes be purchased for about £1,100.

Itinerary   Round trip: 20/30 days

139 ▼   A port in the Gulf of Mexico *USA*   Ecuador
         Colombia   Chile
         Panama   USA
         Peru

Fares

Round trip on bulk carriers: $2100/$3200, or $70 to $105 per day
Round trip on container ships: $2425/$3650, or $80 to $120 per day

---

Itinerary

Round trip: 60/90 days

148 ▼ A port in the Gulf of Mexico *USA*   Thailand
Manila *Philippines*   China
Indonesia   Japan
Malaysia   Hong Kong
occasionally: Singapore   Gulf of Mexico *USA*

Fares

Round trip on bulk carriers: $5600/$7000
Round trip on container ships: $6500/$8000

Itinerary

Round trip: 60/70 days

152 ▼ A port in the Gulf of Mexico *USA*   Maputo *Mozambique*
Cape Town *South Africa*   Beira *Mozambique*
Port Elizabeth *South Africa*   Dar es Salaam *Tanzania*
East London *South Africa*   Mombasa *Kenya*
Durban *South Africa*   Gulf of Mexico *USA*

Fares

Round trip on bulk carriers: $4800/$5200, or $70 to $75 per day
Round trip on container ships: $5500/$6000, or $80 to $85 per day

Marcon Line

Agent in USA:

Freighter World Cruises
180 South Lake Avenue, Suite 335
Pasadena, California 91101 USA
✆ (818) 449 31 06, 🖷 (818) 449 95 73 (international code: 1)

The **Nedlloyd Hong Kong** owned by this Cypriot company follows a unique route between Latin America and the Far East, stopping over in a dozen countries. You can board for South America or for the Far East.

Conditions: maximum age 79

Itinerary

Round trip: 80 days

154 ▼ Puerto Caldera *Costa Rica*
     Manta *Ecuador*
     Chile
     Peru
     Manta *Ecuador*
     Buenaventura *Colombia*
     Puerto Caldera *Costa Rica*
     Japan

Taiwan
Hong Kong
Singapore
Korea
Japan
Lazaro Cardenas *Mexico*
Puerto Caldera *Costa Rica*

Ship and Fares

Nedlloyd Hong Kong:

10 passengers

Facilities: lounge, sauna, pool

Round trip: $7340/$8600, or $91 to $107 per day

Mauritius Shipping Corporation

Coraline
Nova Building
1 Military Road
Port Louis, Mauritius
✆ 242 52 55/241 25 50, 📠 242 52 45 (international code: 230)

Agent in Reunion:

SCOAM, 47 rue Evariste de Parny
Le Port, Reunion
✆ 42 19 45, 📠 43 25 47 (international code: 262)

This is a shipping company belonging to the government of Mauritius and whose passenger-cargo ship, the **Mauritius Pride**, has regular freight and passenger sailings between Mauritius and other destinations in the Indian Ocean.

Itinerary

159 ▼ Port-Louis *Mauritius*
Port-Mathurin *Rodriguez Island*
occasionally: other ports in the
Indian Ocean: Pointe-des-
Galets *Reunion*

Agalega Islands
Ports in Madagascar
Seychelles *and occasionally*:
South Africa

Ship and Fares

Mauritius Pride

Brought into service in 1990, built in Germany, just under 100m long,
with a cruising speed of 13 knots. It can transport both bulk and live-
stock, and can accommodate 248 passengers in seats and 16 passengers
in cabins.

Mauritius   ▶   Rodriguez Island:
MUR650/MUR900/MUR1400 (one way)
Non-Mauritians: prices are increased by 50% for trips to Rodriguez
Reunion   ▶   Mauritius:
480F/720F (low season)
540F/810F (high season), one way
Other voyages: fares on demand

Mediterranean Great Lakes Line

Agent in USA:

Freighter World Cruises
180 South Lake Avenue, Suite 335
Pasadena
California 91101 USA
℡ (818) 449 31 06, ✉ (818) 449 95 73 (international code: 1)

Agent in UK:

The Strand Cruise and Travel Centre
Charing Cross Shopping Concourse
The Strand
London WC2N 4HZ United Kingdom
℡ (0171) 836 6363, ✉ (0171) 497 0078 (international code: 44)

A Croatian company which flies the Cypriot flag, sailing from the Mediterranean to Canada.

Itinerary

Round trip: 18/20 days or 35/40 days

2 ▼ Montreal *Canada*
Liverpool *United Kingdom*
Le Havre *France*
Montreal *Canada*
or:
Montreal *Canada*
Mediterranean ports such as:

Koper *Slovenia*
Trieste *Italy*
Naples/Salerno *Italy*
Genoa *Italy*
Spain
occasionally: Portugal
Montreal *Canada*

Fares

Round trip: Europe ▶ Canada: about $2000, or $100 per day
Round trip: Mediterranean ▶ Canada: $2880/$3500, or $72 to $87 per day

Mediterranean Shipping Company

M.S.C.
18 Chemin Rieu
Geneva, CH 1208 Switzerland
✆ (22) 346 28 22, ✉ (22) 346 13 36 (international code: 41)

Agent in UK:

Medite Shipping
Medite House, Trinity Terminal
The Dock
Felixstowe, Suffolk IP11 8TH
✆ (01394) 67 64 52, ✉ (01394) 67 45 04 (ask for Mrs Archibald)
(international code: 44)

Agent in USA:

Sea the Difference
420 5th Avenue, 8th floor
New York N Y 10018-2702 USA
✆ (212) 764 48 00, ✉ (212) 764 85 92 (ask for Mr Amechazurra)
(international code: 1)

Agent in France:

> Sealiner France
> Quai George V
> 76065 Le Havre/Cedex
> ✆ 35 19 78 00, 🖷 35 19 78 10 (international code: 41)

This is a relatively new Italian company, founded in 1970 by Captain Gianluigi Aponte with just one cargo ship, the **Patricia**. Based in Switzerland, the M.S.C. now has about 50 cargo ships sailing all round the world. Most can accommodate 12 passengers. Its largest cargo ships are the **M.S.C. Lauren** and the **M.S.C. Rita** (40,000 tons), used on the translatlantic route. The **Jade**, 22,000 tons, sails to South Africa.

This company is expanding and is developing a passenger service to South America—a trip which you could combine with a Europe–USA passage to make it more economical.

The cooking on board is Mediterranean and abundant, and Italian wine is served with the meals. There is a sitting room for passengers and certain ships have a swimming pool. Most of the officers and crew are Italian.

> **Nationalities:** Italian officers, international crew
>
> **Conditions:** maximum age 75, minimum age 10

Itinerary

Round trip: 28 days

6 ▼

Antwerp *Belgium*	Boston *Massachusetts USA*
Hamburg *Germany*	New York *USA*
Bremen *Germany*	Baltimore *Maryland USA*
Hamburg *Germany*	Norfolk *Virginia USA*
Felixstowe *United Kingdom*	Antwerp *Belgium*
Le Havre *France*	

Frequency: one departure per week

Fares

For 10 to 13 year olds: 50% discount
For 14 to 20 year olds: 30% discount

Daily prices start from about $115

Round trip (embark and disembark at the same port): $3200

Le Havre	▶	Boston/New York	7/8 days	$1400
Le Havre	▶	Wilmington/Baltimore	11/13 days	$1600

| New York | ▶ | Antwerp/Bremen/Hamburg | 13/16 days | $1800 |
| Wilmington | ▶ | Antwerp/Bremen/Hamburg | 11/14 days | $1600 |

Itinerary
Round trip: 30 days

11 ▼

Antwerp *Belgium*	New Orleans *Louisiana USA*
Rotterdam *Holland*	Houston *Texas USA*
Felixstowe *United Kingdom*	Charleston *South Carolina USA*
Wilmington *USA*	Wilmington *USA*
Charleston *South Carolina USA*	Antwerp *Belgium*
Miami *Florida USA*	

Fares

Antwerp	▶	Charleston	13 days	$1700
Bremen	▶	Miami/Houston/New Orleans	12/17 days	$1800
Houston/New Orleans	▶	Antwerp	12/14 days	$1700
Miami	▶	Antwerp	17 days	$1800

Itinerary
Round trip, from and to New York: about 40 days

38 ▼

Antwerp *Belgium*	Guayaquil *Ecuador*
Rotterdam *Holland*	Callao *Peru*
Bremerhaven *Germany*	Valparaiso *Chile*
Hamburg *Germany*	Arica *Chile*
Felixstowe *United Kingdom*	Callao *Peru*
Charleston *South Carolina USA*	Guayaquil *Ecuador*
(*change vessels*)	Charleston *South Carolina USA*
Panama Canal	

Frequency: one departure per week

Fares

New York	▶	Guayaquil	16 days	$1800
New-York	▶	Callao	19 days	$2200
New-York	▶	Valparaiso	23 days	$2600
Houston	▶	Guayaquil	9 days	$1000
Valparaiso	▶	New York	16 days	$1800
Callao	▶	New York	11 days	$1300
Guayaquil	▶	New York	8 days	$ 900

Itinerary

Round trip: about 28 days

53 ▼ Antwerp *Belgium*
Felixstowe *United Kingdom*
Alexandria *Egypt*
Ashdod *Israel*
Haifa *Israel*

Limassol *Cyprus*
Naples *Italy* (*every other week*)
Livorno *Italy* (*every other week*)
Antwerp *Belgium*

Fares

Round trip (embarking and disembarking at the same port): $3200

Antwerp/Felixstowe ▶	Alexandria/Ashdod	11/14 days	$1500
Antwerp ▶	Haïfa/Limassol	16/17 days	$1700
Alexandria/Ashdod ▶	Antwerp/Felixstowe	14/17 days	$1700
Haïfa/Limassol ▶	Antwerp/Felixstowe	11/13 days	$1300

Itinerary

Round trip: about 41 days

73 ▼ Hamburg *Germany*
Bremen *Germany*
Rotterdam *Holland*
Le Havre *France*
Antwerp *Belgium*
Felixstowe *United Kingdom*

Cape Town *South Africa*
Port Elizabeth *South Africa*
Durban *South Africa*
Cape Town *South Africa*
Le Havre *France*
Antwerp *Belgium*

Frequency: one departure per week

Fares

Round trip: $4500

Le Havre ▶	Cape Town	20 days	$2200
Le Havre ▶	Durban	23 days	$2600
Antwerp ▶	Cape Town	18 days	$2100
Felixstowe ▶	Cape Town	17 days	$2000
Cape Town ▶	Le Havre	14 days	$1600
Cape Town ▶	Felixstowe	17 days	$1600

Itinerary

74 ▼

Antwerp *Belgium*	Port-Louis *Mauritius*
Felixstowe *United Kingdom*	Tamatave *Madagascar*
Dunkirk *France*	*possibly*: Pointe-des-Galets
Rouen *France*	*Reunion*
Nantes *France*	Antwerp *Belgium*
Pointe-des-Galets *Reunion*	

Fares

Antwerp ▶ Indian Ocean   about 26 days $3300
Same prices apply if travelling in the opposite direction

Itinerary

Round trip: about 60 days

75 ▼

Livorno *Italy*	Pointe-des-Galets *Reunion*
Genoa *Italy*	Port-Louis *Mauritius*
Marseilles *France*	Tamatave *Madagascar*
Savona *Italy*	*possibly*: Cape Town *South Africa*
Barcelona *Spain*	Valencia *Spain*
Valencia *Spain*	*possibly*: Barcelona *Spain*
Durban *South Africa*	Livorno *Italy*

Fares

Livorno ▶ Indian Ocean   about 26 days $3300
Same prices apply if travelling in the opposite direction

Itinerary

Round trip: about 53 days

79 ▼

Antwerp *Belgium*	Dar es Salaam *Tanzania*
Felixstowe *United Kingdom*	Mombasa *Kenya*
Suez Canal	Suez Canal
Djibouti	Antwerp *Belgium*

Frequency: one departure per week

Fares

Round trip: $5600

Antwerp/Felixstowe	▶	Djibouti	18/16 days	$2000
Antwerp/Felixstowe	▶	Dar es Salaam	23/21 days	$2700
Antwerp/Felixstowe	▶	Mombasa	27/25 days	$3200
Livorno	▶	Djibouti	10 days	$1100

Itinerary

Round trip: about 84 days

101 ▼ Le Havre *France*
Antwerp *Belgium*
Felixstowe *United Kingdom*
Cape Town *South Africa*
Port Elizabeth *South Africa*
Durban *South Africa*
Fremantle *Australia*
Sydney *Australia*

Melbourne *Australia*
Adelaide *Australia* (*every other week*)
Fremantle *Australia*
Durban *South Africa*
Port Elizabeth *South Africa*
Cape Town *South Africa*
Le Havre *France*

Frequency: one departure per week

Fares

Le Havre	▶	Fremantle	35 days	$3700
Le Havre	▶	Sydney	42 days	$4200
Felixstowe	▶	Fremantle	32 days	$3300
Felixstowe	▶	Sydney	39 days	$3800
Fremantle	▶	Livorno	31 days	$2940
Fremantle	▶	Le Havre	35 days	$2800
Fremantle	▶	Antwerp/Felixstowe	36/38 days	$3000
Sydney	▶	Le Havre	42 days	$3700

Itinerary

Round trip: about 49 days

151 ▼ Charleston *South Carolina USA*
Norfolk *Virginia USA*
Baltimore *Maryland USA*
New York *USA*

Cape Town *South Africa*
Durban *South Africa*
Cape Town *South Africa*
Charleston *South Carolina USA*

Fares

Charleston	▶	Cape Town	23 days	$2750
New York	▶	Cape Town	18 days	$2150
Cape Town	▶	Charleston	18 days	$2150
Cape Town	▶	New York	23 days	$2750

Itinerary

Round trip: 14 days

158 ▼ Durban *South Africa*
Port-Louis *Mauritius*
Pointe-des-Galets *Reunion*

possibly:
Mayotte *Comoros Islands*
Tamatave *Madagascar*
Durban *South Africa*

Fares

Durban	▶	Reunion	3/5 days	$500
Durban	▶	Mauritius	4 days	$600
Durban	▶	Tamatave	7 days	$800
Reunion	▶	Mauritius	2 days	$200
Reunion	▶	Tamatave	3 days	$300
Mauritius	▶	Tamatave	1 day	$100

Itinerary

Round trip: about 40 days

168 ▼ Durban *South Africa*
Fremantle *Australia*
Sydney *Australia*
Melbourne *Australia*

Adelaide *Australia (every other week)*
Fremantle *Australia*
Durban *South Africa*

Fares

Durban	▶	Fremantle	12 days	$1200
Durban	▶	Sydney	18 days	$1700
Sydney	▶	Durban	19 days	$2100
Fremantle	▶	Durban	12 days	$1200

Mineral Shipping

Agent in Germany:

Hamburg-Süd Reiseagentur
Ost-West Str. 59–61
20457 Hamburg Germany
℗ (040) 37 05 155, ✆ (040) 37 05 24 20 (international code: 49)

Agent in USA:

> Freighter World Cruise
> 180 South Lake Avenue #335
> Pasadena
> California 91101 USA
> ✆ (818) 449 31 06, ✇ (818) 449 95 73 (international code: 1)

Agent in UK:

> The Strand Cruise and Travel Centre
> Charing Cross Shopping Concourse
> The Strand
> London WC2N 4HZ United Kingdom
> ✆ (0171) 836 6363, ✇ (0171) 497 0078 (international code: 44)

Agent in Canada:

> Freighter Cruise Service
> Suite 103, 5925 Monkland Avenue,
> Montreal
> Quebec H4A 1G7 Canada
> ✆ (514) 481 04 47 (international code: 1)

The German ships of Mineral Shipping are bulk carriers of the tramp steamer variety. The officers are Croatian. Those who love travelling by cargo ship swear by this company, particularly because of the comfort on board and the warm welcome. Moreover, these bulk carriers often stay several days at port—ideal for those wishing to take advantage of the stopovers.

The ships **Julia** and **Clary** do numerous crossings between the USA, the Mediterranean and Brazil. Two other carriers—**Patty** and **Christiane**—sail the transatlantic route. These comfortable vessels are particularly appreciated by travellers.

Travelling on a tramp steamer implies a certain flexibility, but the rewards are worth the trouble: changes of course, unexpected ports of call, prolonged stopovers—a whiff of the unexpected appreciated by real travellers.

> **Conditions:** maximum age 82
>
> If a journey is shorter than expected, passengers are reimbursed on a pro rata basis. If the voyage is longer, passengers are not charged a supplement

Itinerary

Round trip: about 35 days

8 ▼   Savannah *Georgia USA*   *or* Georgetown *South Carolina*
      Rotterdam/Delfzijl *Holland*   *USA*
      Searsport *Massachusetts USA*   Savannah *Georgia USA*
      Wilmington *North Carolina USA*

Fares

Round trip: DM4000 or DM118 per day

Rotterdam   ▶   Wilmington/Savannah   DM2000

Discounts may be available on winter crossings (however the Atlantic is not always comfortable)

Conditions

Baggage restrictions: 125kg per person. Above this weight: DM4 excess charge per kilo applies.
Dog: DM400; cat: DM300
Cars: DM1300; motorcycles: DM500 (with side-car: DM750)

Itinerary

33 ▼   Various Mediterranean ports,   Yeraniki *Greece*
      amongst them: Various ports in Venezuela and
         Genoa *Italy*   Brazil, including:
         Livorno *Italy*   Munguba (Amazon) *Brazil*
         Ancona *Italy*   Ports in western Europe, *such as*:
         Monfalcone *Italy*   Rotterdam *Holland,* Hamburg
         Porto Vesme *Sardinia*   *Germany*, Bremen *Germany*

Fares

Voyages calculated at a basic price of between $82.50 and $90 per day

Navimag

Navimag
Angelmo 2187
Puerto Montt, Chile
✆ (065) 253 318, 📠 (065) 258 540 (international code: 56)

A spectacular voyage among the islands and straits of Chile's Pacific coast towards the extreme south, the Tierra del Fuego, on board the **Puerto Eden**, a ro-ro able to accommodate 100 passengers.

Itinerary

Round trip: 3 days

143 ▼ *Voyage along the Chilean coastline:* Puerto Montt *Chile*
Puerto Natales *Chile*

Fares: on demand

N. S. B.

N.S.B. Frachtschiff-Touristik
Violenstr. 22
D-28195 Bremen Germany
℡ (0421) 32 16 68, 🖷 (0421) 32 40 89 (international code: 49)

Agent in UK:

The Strand Cruise and Travel Centre
Charing Cross Shopping Concourse
The Strand
London WC2N 4HZ United Kingdom
℡ (0171) 836 6363, 🖷 (0171) 497 0078 (international code: 44)

The N.S.B. shipping company (Niederelbe Schiffahrtsgesellschaft, Bremen) was founded in 1982 following the 'Werftenverbund' of Bremen. A large number of the ships it uses are rented to large international shipping companies (for periods longer than three years). Other ships are being built for the company itself.

The company has taken passengers on board since 1989. It opened its own office in Bremen to have more control over its worldwide itineraries; you can ring to find out about departures over the following two weeks. As with most container ships, stopovers only last between 6 and 12 hours, except in Australia, Africa, India and South America, where they last from one to three days.

Average price per day: DM110 to DM200, depending on the vessel. Discounts for 'second' passengers. No limit on personal luggage

Nationalities: German officers, international crew

Facilities: most of the vessels have a sauna, gym, video lounge, laundry room and a swimming pool.

Conditions: maximum age 79, minimum age 15

Itinerary

Round trip: about 30 days

4 ▼ Salerno *Italy*
Livorno *Italy*
Genoa *Italy*
Valencia *Spain*

Cadiz *Spain*
Lisbon *Portugal*
Montreal *Canada*
Salerno *Italy*

Ship and Fares

Canmar Intrepid

Built in 1984, 33,857 tons, 2 passengers, 1 owner's cabin with bedroom and sitting room, 1 single cabin. Cabins have shower/wc.

Fare per day: DM160 to DM220

Itinerary

Round trip: about 44 days

14 ▼ La Spezia *Italy*
Miami *Florida USA*
Houston *Texas USA*
New Orleans *Louisiana USA*

Valencia *Spain*
Barcelona *Spain*
La Spezia *Italy*

Ship and Fares

Contship England

Built in 1985, 13,350 tons, 2 passengers, 1 owner's cabin with bedroom and sitting room, 1 single cabin. Cabins have shower/wc.

Fare per day: DM150 to DM180

Itinerary

Round trip: about 39 days

52 ▼ Hamburg *Germany*
Rotterdam *Holland*
Antwerp *Belgium*
Tunis *Tunisia*
Alexandria *Egypt*
Beirut *Lebanon*
Tartus *Syria*

Istanbul *Turkey*
Salonika *Greece*
Izmir *Turkey*
Salerno *Italy*
Felixstowe *United Kingdom*
Hamburg *Germany*

Ship and Fares

Kairo

Built in 1994, 20,283 tons, 4 passengers, 1 owner's cabin with bedroom and sitting room, 1 double cabin with bed, sofabed, sitting room. All cabins have shower/wc.

Fare per day: DM160/DM200

Itinerary

Round trip: about 62 days

64 ▼   Hamburg *Germany*
Antwerp *Belgium*
Rotterdam *Holland*
Felixstowe *United Kingdom*
Le Havre *France*
Dakar *Senegal*
Conakry *Guinea*
Freetown *Sierra Leone*
Abidjan *Ivory Coast*
Tema *Ghana*
Lomé *Togo*

Cotonou *Benin*
Lagos *Nigeria*
Libreville *Gabon*
Douala *Cameroon*
Abidjan *Ivory Coast*
Dakar *Senegal*
Leixoes *Portugal*
Antwerp *Belgium*
Hamburg *Germany*
Tilbury *United Kingdom*

Ship and Fares

Buxmerchant

Built in 1989, 26,250 tons, 11 passengers, 1 owner's cabin with bedroom and sitting room, 4 double cabins with sitting room, 1 single cabin. All cabins have shower/wc.

Fare per day: DM120 to DM210

Itinerary

Round trip: about 51 days

81 ▼   Hamburg *Germany*
Antwerp *Belgium*
Suez Canal
Dubai *United Arab Emirates*
Karachi *Pakistan*

Bombay *India*
Suez Canal
Felixstowe *United Kingdom*
Hamburg *Germany*

Ships and Fares

Contship Asia, Contship Pacific, Contship Atlantic

Built 1993/4, 22,500 tons, 10 passengers each vessel, 1 owner's cabin with bedroom and sitting room, 3 double cabins with bedroom and sitting room, 1 single cabin (can also be used as a double). All cabins have shower/wc.

Round trip: DM6120/DM8160, or DM120 to DM160 per day

| Hamburg | ▶ | Karachi | about 22 days | DM2640/DM3520 |
| Hamburg | ▶ | Bombay | about 27 days | DM3420/DM4320 |

Itinerary

Round trip: about 64 days

83 ▼
Algeciras *Spain*	Halifax *Canada*
Malta	New York *New York USA*
Suez Canal	Baltimore *Maryland USA*
Jeddah *Saudi Arabia*	Miami *Florida USA*
Jebel Ali *Sudan*	Houston *Texas USA*
Bombay *India*	Charleston *South Carolina USA*
Jeddah *Saudi Arabia*	Baltimore *Maryland USA*
Suez Canal	New York *New York USA*
Malta	Algeciras *Spain*
Algeciras *Spain*	

Ship and Fares

Sea Initiative

Built in 1993, 45,470 tons, 10 passengers, 1 owner's cabin with bedroom and sitting room, 3 double cabins with bedroom and sitting room, 1 single cabin (can be used as double). All cabins have shower/wc.

Fare per day: DM130 to DM220

Itinerary

Round trip: about 63 days

86 ▼   Hamburg *Germany*

Zeebrugge *Belgium*

Southampton *United Kingdom*

Algeciras *Spain*

Suez Canal

Singapore

Hong Kong

Kaohsiung *Taiwan*

Pusan *South Korea*

Kaohsiung *Taiwan*

Hong Kong

Singapore

Suez Canal

Algeciras *Spain*

Southampton *United Kingdom*

Rotterdam *Holland*

Bremen *Germany*

Hamburg *Germany*

Ship and Fares

Maersk Antwerp

Built 1994, 45,470 tons, 10 passengers, 1 owner's cabin with bedroom and sitting room, 3 double cabins with bedroom and sitting room, 1 single cabin (can also be used as a double). All cabins have shower/wc.

Fare per day: DM120 to DM200

Itinerary

Round trip: about 63 days

87 ▼   Hamburg *Germany*

Rotterdam *Holland*

Felixstowe *United Kingdom*

Malta

Suez Canal

Jeddah *Saudi Arabia*

Dubai *United Arab Emirates*

Colombo *Sri Lanka*

Singapore

Hong Kong

Pusan *South Korea*

Keelung (Chilung) *Taiwan*

Hong Kong

Singapore

Colombo *Sri Lanka*

Suez Canal

Malta

Algeciras *Spain*

Hamburg *Germany*

Ship and Fares

Sea Endeavour, Sea Progress

Built 1993/4, 45,470 tons, 10 passengers, 1 owner's cabin with bedroom and sitting room, 3 double cabins with bedroom and sitting room, 1 single cabin (can be used as a double). All cabins have shower/wc.

Fare per day: DM130 to DM163

Itinerary

Round trip: about 60 days

88 ▼ Hamburg *Germany*   Pusan *South Korea*
       Isle of Grain *United Kingdom*   Keelung *Taiwan*
       Rotterdam *Holland*   Kaohsiung *Taiwan*
       Antwerp *Belgium*   Hong Kong
       Damietta *Egypt*   Singapore
       Jeddah *Saudi Arabia*   Colombo *Sri Lanka*
       Fujairah *United Arab Emirates* Damietta *Egypt*
       Singapore   Le Havre *France*
       Hong Kong   Hamburg *Germany*

Ships and Fares

Ville de Libra, Ville de Sagitta, Ville de Vela

Built in 1994, 42,673 tons, 8 pasengers each vessel, 1 owner's cabin with bedroom and sitting room, 1 luxury double cabin with bedroom and sitting room, 2 double cabins with bedroom. All cabins have shower/wc.

Fare per day: DM180 to DM220

Itinerary

Round trip: about 63 days

91 ▼ La Spezia *Italy*   Pusan *South Korea*
       Fos-sur-Mer *France*   Hong Kong
       Suez Canal   Singapore
       Jeddah *Saudi Arabia*   Jeddah *Saudi Arabia*
       Khor Fakkan *United Arab* Suez Canal
         Emirates   La Spezia *Italy*
       Singapore

Ships and Fares

Singapore Senator

Built 1989, 26,250 tons, 12 passengers, 1 owner's cabin with bedroom and sitting room, 4 double cabins with bedroom and sitting room, 1 single cabin (can be used as a double). All cabins have shower/wc.

Fare per day: DM110 to DM175

Itinerary

94 ▼   Hamburg *Germany*
      Zeebrugge *Belgium*
      Southampton *United Kingdom*
      Algeciras *Spain*
      Malta
      Suez Canal
      Singapore
      Yantian *China*
      Hong Kong

Singapore
Colombo *Sri Lanka*
Jeddah *Saudi Arabia*
Suez Canal
Malta
Algeciras *Spain*
Rotterdam *Holland*
Hamburg *Germany*

Ships and Fares

Mersk Antwerp

Built 1994, 75,470 tons, 8 passengers, 1 large double cabin, 3 standard double cabins, 1 single cabin. All cabins have shower/wc.

Fare per day: DM180 (large double cabin); DM160 (standard double cabin); DM130 (single cabin)

Itineraries

97 ▼   Hamburg *Germany*
      Rotterdam *Holland*
      La Spezia *Italy*
      Suez Canal
      Melbourne *Australia*
      Fremantle Australia

Suez Canal
La Spezia *Italy*
Zeebrugge *Belgium*
Tilbury *United Kingdom*
Hamburg *Germany*

98 ▼   Hamburg *Germany*
      Rotterdam *Holland*
      Barcelona Spain
      La Spezia *Italy*
      Suez Canal
      Melbourne *Australia*
      Sydney *Australia*

Melbourne *Australia*
Fremantle *Australia*
Suez Canal
La Spezia *Italy*
Zeebrugge *Belgium*
Tilbury *United Kingdom*

Ships and Fares

Contship Ipswich, Contship Germany, Contship Barcelona, Contship France, Contship Jork, Contship Europe

Built 1990–5, 22,500 tons, 10 passengers each vessel, 1 owner's cabin with bedroom and sitting room, 3 double cabins with bedroom and sit ting room, 1 single cabin (can be used as a double). All cabins have shower/wc.

Round trip: DM10520/DM15140, or DM120 to DM175 per day

Hamburg	▶ Melbourne	about 33 days	DM4400/DM6215
Hamburg	▶ Auckland	about 41 days	DM5360/DM7000
Fremantle	▶ Hamburg	about 32 days	DM4280/DM6040

Itineraries

Round trip: about 98 days

127 ▼ *Round-the-world voyage*:
Hamburg *Germany*
Rotterdam *Holland*
Dunkirk France
Le Havre *France*
New York *USA*
Norfolk *Virginia USA*
Savannah *Georgia USA*
Panama Canal
Papeete *Tahiti*
Noumea New Caledonia
Auckland *New Zealand*
Melbourne *Australia*
Sydney *Australia*
Keelung *Taiwan*
Hong Kong
Singapore
Suez Canal
Port Said *Egypt*
Salerno *Italy*
Savona *Italy*
Felixstowe *United Kingdom*
Hamburg *Germany*

128 ▼ *Round-the-world voyage*:
Hamburg *Germany*
Rotterdam *Holland*
Barcelona *Spain*
Fos-sur-Mer *France*
Suez Canal
Melbourne *Australia*
Sydney *Australia*
Auckland *New Zealand*
Keelung *Taiwan*
Hong Kong
Singapore
Suez Canal
Port Said *Egypt*
Salerno *Italy*
Savona *Italy*
Felixstowe *United Kingdom*
Hamburg *Germany*

Ships and Fares

Contship Italy, Contship La Spezia, Contship Singapore

Built 1990 and 1994, 22,500 tons, 10 passengers each vessel, 1 owner's cabin with bedroom and sitting room, 3 double cabins with bedroom and sitting room, 1 single cabin (can be used as a double). All cabins have shower/wc.

Round trip: DM11760/DM15680, or DM120 to DM175 per day

Itinerary   Round trip: about 62 days

132 ▼ Hamburg *Germany*   Kobe *Japan*
Felixstowe *United Kingdom*   Pusan *South Korea*
Rotterdam *Holland*   Kaohsiung *Taiwan*
Port Said *Egypt*   Hong Kong
Suez Canal   Singapore
Singapore   Suez Canal
Hong Kong   Port Said *Egypt*
Kaohsiung *Taiwan*   Rotterdam *Holland*
Yokohama *Japan*   Hamburg *Germany*

Ships and Fares

Sea Progress

Built 1993, 75,470 tons, 8 passengers, 1 large double cabin, 3 standard double cabins, 1 single cabin. All cabins have shower/wc.

Fare per day: DM180 (large double cabin); DM160 (standard double cabin); DM130 (single cabin)

Itinerary

Round trip: about 47 days

134 ▼ New Orleans *Louisiana USA*

Houston *Texas USA*
Puerto Cabello *Venezuela*
La Guaira *Venezuela*
Recife *Brazil*
Rio de Janeiro *Brazil*
Santos *Brazil*
Buenos Aires *Argentina*
Montevideo *Uruguay*
Rio Grande *Brazil*

Itajai *Brazil*
Paranagua *Brazil*
Santos *Brazil*
Fortaleza *Brazil*
Salvador *Brazil*
San Juan *Puerto Rico*
Veracruz *Mexico*
Tampico *Mexico*
New Orleans *Louisiana USA*
Houston *Texas USA*

Ship and Fares

Doria

Built in 1985, 13,350 tons, 2 passengers, 1 owner's cabin with bedroom and sitting room, 1 single cabin. Cabins have shower/wc.

Fare per day: DM120 to DM160

Itinerary

Round trip: about 92 days

161 ▼ Singapore

Hong Kong
Keelung *Taiwan*
Pusan *South Korea*
Kobe *Japan*
Yokohama *Japan*
Lazaro Cardenas *Mexico*
Manta *Ecuador*
Callao *Peru*
Iquique *Chile*
San Antonio *Chile*

Arica *Peru*
Callao *Peru*
Manta *Ecuador*
Buenaventura *Colombia*
Port Caldera *Chile*
Yokohama *Japan*
Kobe *Japan*
Pusan *South Korea*
Keelung *Taiwan*
Hong Kong
Singapore

Ship and Fares

Buxwind

Built in 1986, 22,500 tons, 4 passengers, 1 owner's cabin with bedroom and sitting room, 1 double cabin. Cabins have shower/wc.

Fare per day: DM140 to DM160

Itinerary

Round trip: about 35 days

162 ▼ Pusan *South Korea*
      Hong Kong
      Kaohsiung *Taiwan*
      Pusan *South Korea*

Seattle *Washington USA*
Portland *Oregon USA*
Seattle *Washington USA*
Pusan *South Korea*

Ship and Fares

Hyundai Tacoma

Built in 1993, 32,700 tons, 6 passengers, 1 luxury double cabin with sitting room, 1 standard double cabin, 1 double cabin. All cabins have shower/wc.

Fare per day: DM180

Itinerary

Round trip: about 91 days

163 ▼ Pusan *South Korea*
      Keelung *Taiwan*
      Hong Kong
      Singapore
      Buenos Aires *Argentina*
      Montevideo *Uruguay*
      Rio Grande *Brazil*
      Sao Francisco do Sul *Brazil*
      Paranagua *Brazil*

Santos *Brazil*
Salvador *Brazil*
Durban *South Africa*
Singapore
Manila *Philippines*
Hong Kong
Keelung *Taiwan*
Pusan *South Korea*

Ship and Fares

Nedlloyd Salvador

Built in 1994, 20,283 tons, 4 passengers, 1 owner's cabin with bedroom and sitting room, 1 double cabin with bedroom and sitting room. All cabins have shower/wc.

Fare per day: DM140 to DM160

Round trip: about 96 days

164 ▼ Pusan *South Korea*
    Kobe *Japan*
    Yokohama *Japan*
    Lazaro Cardenas *Mexico*
    Callao *Peru*
    Iquique *Chile*
    San Antonio *Chile*
    Arica *Peru*
    Ilo *Peru*
    Callao *Peru*
    Manta *Ecuador*
    Buenaventura *Colombia*
    Yokohama *Japan*
    Nagoya *Japan*
    Kobe *Japan*
    Pusan *South Korea*
    Keelung *Taiwan*

Hong Kong
Singapore
Durban *South Africa*
Cape Town *South Africa*
Montevideo *Uruguay*
Buenos Aires *Argentina*
Sao Francisco do Sul *Brazil*
Paranagua *Brazil*
Santos *Brazil*
Vitoria *Brazil*
Durban *South Africa*
Colombo *Sri Lanka*
Singapore
Hong Kong
Keelung *Taiwan*
Pusan *South Korea*

Ship and Fares

Nedlloyd Sao Paulo

Built in 1994, 283 tons, 4 passengers, 1 owner's cabin with bedroom and sitting room, 1 double cabin with bedroom and sitting room. All cabins have shower/wc.

Fare per day: DM140 to DM160

P & O Containers

Agent in UK:

The Strand Cruise and Travel Centre
Charing Cross Shopping Concourse
The Strand
London WC2N 4HZ United Kingdom
✆ (0171) 836 6363, 🖷 (0171) 497 0078 (international code: 44)

This British company, part of the P&O Group, operate two very comfortable container vessels which sail to South Africa, Australia and New Zealand. Accommodation is provided for 6 passengers on the **City of Durban**, which sails year round to South Africa, and for 8 passengers on the **Palliser Bay**, which sails year round to Australia and New Zealand.

Conditions: maximum age 80

Itinerary

Round trip: 44 days

70 ▼   Tilbury *United Kingdom*
        Cape Town *South Africa*
        Port Elizabeth *South Africa*
        Durban *South Africa*

Port Elizabeth *South Africa*
Cape Town *South Africa*
Tilbury *United Kingdom*

Ship and Fares

City of Durban

Built in 1978, 52,055 tons, 6 passengers in 3 large double cabins each with shower/wc, lounge with TV/video, swimming pool

UK   ▶   South Africa/South Africa   ▶   UK: £1100–£1800

Itinerary

Round trip: about 80 days

99 ▼   Tilbury *United Kingdom*
        Rotterdam *Holland*
        Cape Town *South Africa*
        Fremantle *Australia*
        Adelaide *Australia*
        Burnie *Australia*
        Melbourne *Australia*
        Sydney *Australia*

Auckland *New Zealand*
Wellington *New Zealand*
Lyttleton *New Zealand*
Port Chalmers *New Zealand*
Lisbon *Portugal*
Zeebrugge *Belgium*
Tilbury *United Kingdom*

Ship and Fares

Palliser Bay

Built in 1977, 44,150 tons, 8 passengers in 1 owner's cabin with sitting room and bedroom, shower/wc, 3 double cabins with shower/wc, lounge with TV/video, swimming pool

UK ▶ Australia/New Zealand: £1900–£2375
New Zealand/Australia ▶ UK: £1900–£2375

Palau Shipping Company

Carolineship
P.O. Box 6000
Koror, Palau Islands
Western Caroline Islands 96940

The **Micronesia Princess**, from the Palau shipping company, links three Micronesian islands. The cargo ship, built in 1965, can accommodate 12 passengers.

Itinerary

169 ▼ *Inter-island voyages in*   Yap
Micronesia: Guam *Mariana Islands*
Koror *Palau Islands*   Koror *Palau Islands*

Fare and conditions: not supplied

Peter Dohle

Agent in UK:

The Strand Cruise and Travel Centre
Charing Cross Shopping Concourse
The Strand
London WC2N 4HZ United Kingdom
✆ (0171) 836 6363, ✇ (0171) 497 0078 (international code: 44)

The German company Peter Dohle, associated with Baum Shipping, operates in the Mediterranean and South America.

Nationalities: German officers, international crew
Conditions: maximum age 75

Ships

Atlantic Express

Built in 1991, 14,867 tons, 8 passengers, 2 double cabins, 4 singles

Brasil Express

Built in 1992, 14,867 tons, 4 passengers, one double cabin, 2 single cabins

Facilities: both boats have a video lounge and pool

Itinerary

Round trip: about 55 days

30 ▼	Tilbury *United Kingdom*	Bilbao *Spain*
	Hamburg *Germany*	Santos *Brazil*
	Bremen *Germany*	Buenos Aires *Argentina*
	Rotterdam *Holland*	Montevideo *Uruguay*
	Antwerp *Belgium*	Sao Francisco do Sul *Brazil*
	Le Havre *France*	Tilbury *United Kingdom*

Fares

Round trip: £3560/£3850, or £64 to £70 per day

Tilbury	▶	Santos	22 days	£1840/£1954
Tilbury	▶	Buenos Aires	26 days	£2050/£2185
Tilbury	▶	Montevideo	28 days	£2155/£2300

Polish Ocean Lines

P.O.L. Passenger Department
Dluga 76
80-831 Gdansk Poland
✆ (58) 31 48 51, ✆ (58) 31 59 64 (international code: 48)

In UK:

Gdynia America Lines
238 City Road
London EC1V 2QL United Kingdom
✆ (0171) 251 3389, ✆ (0171) 250 3625 (international code: 44)

In USA:

Gdynia America Line
South Plainfield
1001 Durham Avenue
N.J. 07080-2303, USA
✆ (908) 412 6000 (international code: 1)

Agent in France:

CIFED
11 rue Richepance
75008 Paris France
✆ (1) 42 60 36 08, ✉ (1) 47 03 93 10 (international code: 33)

Polish Ocean Lines succeeded the Polish company Gdynia America Shipping Lines in 1951 and has always welcomed passengers on its vessels.

Today it is one of the largest companies to transport passengers, as it offers numerous voyages, and at the lowest rates. It is one of the first companies to contact if you want to travel at a competitive price. It offers some trips at US$20 or 30 per day, which is frankly unbeatable.

One word of advice: don't hesitate to go (by cargo ship) to Gdynia, on the Baltic. It is the registration port of P.O.L. and it is an attractive and little-known region.

The cabins on the Polish cargo ships are perhaps not as luxurious as some top-of-the-range cargo ships, but the atmosphere on board is friendly and convivial. There is a guaranteed change of scenery. Most of the officers speak English. Polish cuisine has some nice surprises in store.

Moreover the P.O.L. is a company which has maintained a service for passengers against all the odds, even when other companies closed their cabins to passengers.

Some of its ships have recently been sold or rented to other companies which unfortunately chose to exclude passengers—which explains the closing of the transatlantic route and the route to southeast Asia and Vietnam.

It was also P.O.L. which offered, until the end of the 1980s, one of the last transatlantic services on board the passenger liner **Stefan Batory**, a ship with old-fashioned charm and an unforgettable atmosphere.

Nationalities: Polish officers and crew

Conditions: maximum age 75
Children under 12 years: 50% discount
Weight restrictions: 125 kilos

Port tax: For a one way trip: $40
For a round trip: $80

Single cabin supplement: 10%

Itinerary

24 ▼ A western European port   Santo Tomas de Castilla
La Guaira *Venezuela*   *Guatemala*
Cartagena *Colombia*   Veracruz *Mexico*
Panama   New Orleans/Houston *Texas*
Puerto Limon *Costa Rica*   *USA*
                            A western European port

Frequency: monthly sailings

Fares

Round trip: $3000, or about $37.50 per day

Europe	▶	La Guaira/Puerto Cabello	(20/22 days)	$ 950
Europe	▶	Cartagena		$1050
Europe	▶	Costa Rica	(about 24 days)	$1100
Europe	▶	Guatemala		$1200
Europe	▶	Veracruz		$1300
Europe	▶	New Orleans/Houston		$1450

Itinerary

32 ▼ Gdynia *Poland*   Santos *Brazil*
A western European port   Rio de Janeiro *Brazil*
Buenos Aires *Argentina*   Salvador *Brazil*
Montevideo *Uruguay*   A western European port

Frequency: monthly sailings

Fares

Round trip: $3000, or about $35 per day

Gdynia/western European port	▶	Buenos Aires	$ 800
Gdynia/western European port	▶	Montevideo	$1000
Gdynia/western European port	▶	Santos	$1200
Gdynia/western European port	▶	Rio de Janeiro	$1300
Gdynia/western European port	▶	Salvador	$1400

Itinerary

36 ▼ Gdynia *Poland*
A western European port
Panama Canal
Guayaquil *Ecuador*
Callao *Peru*
Arica *Chile*

Antofagasta *Chile*
Valparaiso *Chile*
Straits of Magellan
Brazil
A western European port
Gdynia *Poland*

Frequency: one departure every 20 days

Fares

Round trip: $3000, or about $40 per day

A western European port	▶	Panama Canal	$ 950
A western European port	▶	Guayaquil	$1050
A western European port	▶	Callao	$1200
A western European port	▶	Valparaiso	$1550
A western European port	▶	Arica	$1700

Itinerary

Round trip: about 30 days

49 ▼ Gdynia *Poland*
A western European port
Casablanca *Morocco*
Valletta *Malta*
Tunis *Tunisia*

Alexandria *Egypt*
Lattakia *Syria*
Limassol *Cyprus*
A western European port
Gdynia *Poland*

Fares

Round trip: $920, or $30 per day

A western European port	▶	Casablanca	$410
A western European port	▶	Valetta	$520
A western European port	▶	Alexandria	$635
A western European port	▶	Lattakia	$695
A western European port	▶	Limassol	$750

Itinerary

Round trip: 60/70 days

66 ▼ Szczecin *Poland*   Lomé *Togo*
       A western European port   Cotonou *Benin*
       Dakjar *Senegal*   Douala *Cameroon*
       Banjul *Gambia*   Lagos *Nigeria*
       Abidjan *Ivory Coast*   A western European port
       Tema *Ghana*   Szczecin *Poland*

Fares

Round trip: $1700, or about $28 per day

A western European port	▶	Banjul	$500
A western European port	▶	Tema	$600
A western European port	▶	Abidjan	$650
A western European port	▶	Lagos	$700

Itinerary

Round trip: 120/140 days

76 ▼ Antwerp *Belgium*   Jeddah *Saudi Arabia*
       Suez *Egypt*   Karachi *Pakistan*
       Hodeïda *Yemen*   Mombasa *Kenya*
       Massauo *Ethiopia*   Comoros Islands
       Port Sudan *Sudan*   Antwerp *Belgium*

Frequency: monthly sailings

Fares

Round trip: $4500, or $35 per day

Antwerp	▶	Hodeïda	$650
Antwerp	▶	Massauo	$670
Antwerp	▶	Port Sudan	$700
Antwerp	▶	Jeddah	$1160
Antwerp	▶	Karachi	$950
Antwerp	▶	Mombasa	$1250
Antwerp	▶	Comoros Islands	$1450

Itinerary   Round trip: 7 days

121 ▼   Felixstowe *United Kingdom*   Copenhagen *Denmark*
        Copenhagen *Denmark*   Felixstowe *United Kingdom*
        Gdynia *Poland*

Fares

        Round trip: £230

Projex Line

Agents in Germany:

        Hamburg-Süd Reiseagentur
        Ost-West Str. 59–61
        20457 Hamburg Germany
        ✆ (040) 37 05 155, ✉ (040) 37 05 24 20 (international code: 49)

        Frachtschiff-Touristik (Captain Peter Zylmann)
        Exhöft 12
        24404 Maasholm Germany
        ✆ 0 4642 60 68, ✉ 0 4642 67 67 (international code: 49)

Agent in UK:

        The Strand Cruise and Travel Centre
        Charing Cross Shopping Concourse
        The Strand
        London WC2N 4HZ United Kingdom
        ✆ (0171) 836 6363, ✉ (0171) 497 0078 (international code: 44)

Itinerary   Round trip: about 38 days

40 ▼   Felixstowe *United Kingdom*   Beirut *Lebanon*
        Hamburg/Bremen *Germany*   Mersin *Turkey*
        Rotterdam *Holland*   Istanbul *Turkey*
        Antwerp *Belgium*   Salonika *Greece*
        Tunis *Tunisia*   Izmir *Turkey*
        Alexandria *Egypt*   Salerno *Italy*
        Port Said *Egypt*   Felixstowe *United Kingdom*

Ship and Fares

Contship Egypt

Formerly the **Harmony**, built in 1994

Round trip: DM3990/DM6180, or DM105 to DM162 per day

Itinerary

Round trip: about 9 weeks

92 ▼   La Spezia *Italy*

La Spezia *Italy*	Singapore
Fos-sur-Mer *France*	Pusan *South Korea*
Valencia *Spain*	Kaohsiung *Taiwan*
Larnaka *Cyprus*	Hong Kong
Suez Canal	Singapore
Jeddah *Saudi Arabia*	Jeddah *Saudi Arabia*
Khor Fakkan *United Arab Emirates*	Suez Canal
	La Spezia *Italy*

Fares

Round trip: DM8600/DM10,776, or DM136 to DM170 per day

La Spezia	▶ Singapore	about 4 weeks	DM4050/DM5036
La Spezia	▶ Pusan	5 to 6 weeks	DM5090/DM6348
Singapore	▶ La Spezia	17/18 days	DM2620/DM3232

Relais Nordik

In Canada:

Relais Nordik
205 Léonidas
Rimouski
Quebec G5L 2T5 Canada
℡ (418) 723 87 87, ✉ (418) 722 93 07 (international code: 1)

Agent in UK:

The Strand Cruise and Travel Centre
Charing Cross Shopping Concourse
The Strand
London WC2N 4HZ United Kingdom
℡ (0171) 836 6363, ✉ (0171) 497 0078 (international code: 44)

This is a Canadian company which for some time has maintained the link between Rimouski, in the estuary of the St Lawrence river, and the small ports to the extreme east of Quebec, in the strait of Belle Isle separating Newfoundland from the continent. The ship belongs to a private company but it is subsidized up to 60% by the government so that the tickets are not too expensive and do not penalize the inhabitants of these remote regions.

The coaster **Nordik Express** can accommodate up to 60 passengers and includes about 15 ports of call. You can hire a bicycle and take it on board to take better advantage of the stopovers. You can also get off at a port of call and pick the vessel up again a few days later.

It is also a spectacular way of seeing blue whales, belugas and seals by day and aurora borealis at night. In April the Gulf is still an ice field, and a spectacular voyage is guaranteed. Book well in advance.

Itinerary

Round trip: 7 days

155 ▼ *Voyage along the east coast of Canada*:

Rimouski	Blanc-Sablon
Sept-Iles	Vieux-Fort
Port Menier (Ile d'Anticosti)	St Augustin
Havre-St-Pierre	La Tabatière
Baie Johan Beetz	Tête-à-la-Baleine
Natashquan	Harrington Harbour
Kegashka	La Romaine
La Romaine	Kegashka
Harrington Harbour	Natashquan
Tête-à-la-Baleine	Baie Johan Beets
La Tabatière	Havre-St-Pierre
St Augustin	Port-Menier
Vieux-Fort	Sept-Iles
	Rimouski

Frequency: weekly sailings between April and October

Ship and Fares

Nordik Express

1619 tons, 60 passengers, 6 cabins with a total of 20 couchettes, 10 cabins with a total of 40 couchettes

Facilities: covered observatory, lounge, video room, cafeteria, restaurant

Couchette (per night): CAN $31
Meal prices: CAN $13
Round trip (set fare including couchette and meals):
CAN $740, or CAN $105 per day
Rimouski ▶ Blanc-Sablon (4 days):
Fixed fare: CAN $400
Passage excluding couchette and meals: CAN $200
Reduced rates apply to Canadians under the age of 12 or over 65
Cars, bicycles and motorcycles can be taken on board

Safmarine

BP Centre, Thibault Square
Cape Town 8001
PO Box 27 & 2171
Cape Town 8000 South Africa
℡ (021) 408 69 11 (ask for Dominique Gross)
🖷 (021) 408 65 13 (international code: 27)

Agent in UK:

Pathfinder Windward Terminal
Herbert Walker Avenue
Southampton
Hampshire SO1 OXP United Kingdom
℡ (01703) 334415/333388 (ask for captain Dick Hellyer)
🖷 (01703) 714059 (international code: 44)

Founded in 1946, Union-Castle/Safmarine used to transport post between the UK and South Africa. In 1977 its postal boat, the **S.A. Vaal**, made her last crossing.

Today, four white container ships built in France (known as 'Big Whites') make up the fleet of this South African company (Safmarine is an abbreviation of South African Marine Corporation). They sail regularly between Great Britain and South Africa, and rotate every nine days (27 voyages per year each way).

The service on board is top-class.

Nationalities: South African and British officers and crew

Ships

S.A. Winterberg, S.A. Waterberg, .S.A. Helderberg, S.A. Sederberg

All four built between 1977 and 1978, 55000 tons, 10 passengers, 5 double cabins

Facilities: library, video lounge, launderette, steward, lifts, TV in each cabin

Conditions: minimum age 2; no maximum age, but a medical certificate is required for all passengers

Itinerary

One way: 15/16 days

71 ▼ Tilbury *United Kingdom*
Le Havre *France*
Cape Town *South Africa*
Port Elizabeth/Durban
South Africa

Zeebrugge *Belgium*/Le Havre
France
Tilbury *United Kingdom*

Fares

Tilbury ▶ Cape Town about 17 days:
$1800/$2400, or $105 to $140 per day
Same prices apply when travelling from Cape Town to Tilbury
Tilbury ▶ Durban: $2100/$4350
Same prices apply when travelling from Durban to Tilbury

Conditions: children under 12: 50% discount
Discounts in low season (Oct–Jan to the north, May–Aug to the south):
Tilbury ▶ Cape Town: $1200/$1600
Tilbury ▶ Durban: $1500/$2100
Same price in the other direction

Frequency: one departure approximately every 9 days

St Helena Shipping Company

Curnow Shipping
The Shipyard, Portleven
Helston
Cornwall TR13 9JA United Kingdom
℡ (01326) 56 34 34, ℻ (01326) 56 43 47 (international code: 44)

France:

r et Voyages
3 rue Tronchet
75008 Paris France
✆ (1) 44 51 01 68, 📠 (1) 40 07 12 72 (international code: 33)

Agent in South Africa:

St Helena Line Pty. Ltd., 2nd floor
B.P. Centre, Thibault Square
Cape Town, South Africa
✆ (021) 25 11 65, 📠 (021) 21 74 85 (international code: 27)

St Helena is a natural port of call between Great Britain and South Africa. The island, lost in the middle of the south Atlantic 1200 miles from the African coast, cannot be reached by aeroplane for the simple reason that it does not have an airport. This explains why there is still a passenger-cargo service on this route, the only link between the British island and the rest of the world.

Before that the service was operated by Union-Castle (*see* Safmarine, p.190). For the last 15 years Curnow Shipping has maintained the link with a passenger-cargo ship built in 1990 which is currently winning acclaim: the **RMS St Helena**. 'RMS' means 'Royal Mail Ship', as she conveys the post to the island made famous by the exile and death of Napoleon (said today to have been poisoned by those close to him).

The **St Helena** is a rare pearl, and operates one of the last regular services of a passenger-carrying cargo vessel. Numerous enthusiastic articles have been written about her. A relic from another age, she presents all the characteristics of a small elegant liner, accommodating 128 passengers.

Nationalities: British and St Helenian officers, St Helenian crew
Conditions: no age limit (doctor on board)

Itinerary

Each way: about 28 days

69 ▼   Cardiff *United Kingdom*   (*once a year*: Tristan da Cunha)
Tenerife *Canary Islands*   St Helena
Ascension Island   Ascension Island
St Helena   St Helena
Ascension Island   Tenerife *Canary Islands*
St Helena   *occasionally*: Banjul *Gambia*
Cape Town *South Africa*   Cardiff *United Kingdom*

Note: For voyages to the north, and sometimes to the south, passengers are obliged to disembark at St Helena and sometimes stay there for up to 8 days at their own expense (arranged by the company).

Once a year the ship sails from Cape Town to Tristan da Cunha.

Fares

Cardiff ▶	Tenerife	5 days	£ 180/£ 596
Cardiff ▶	Ascencion Island	12 days	£ 751/£1513
Cardiff ▶	St Helena	14 days	£ 390/£1606
Cardiff ▶	Cape Town	21/25 days	£1230/£2480

Transeste

Agent in France:

Mer et Voyages
3 rue Tronchet
75008 Paris France
✆ (1) 44 51 01 68, 📠 (1) 40 07 12 72

Agent in UK:

The Strand Cruise and Travel Centre
Charing Cross Shopping Concourse
The Strand
London WC2N 4HZ United Kingdom
✆ (0171) 836 6363, 📠 (0171) 497 0078 (international code: 44)

Agents in Germany:

Frachtschiff-Touristik (Captain Peter Zylmann)
Exhöft 12
24404 Maasholm Germany
✆ 0 4642 60 68, 📠 0 4642 67 67 (international code: 49)

Hamburg-Süd Reiseagentur
Ost-West Str. 59–61
20457 Hamburg Germany
✆ (040) 37 05 155, 📠 (040) 37 05 24 20 (international code: 49)

Nationalities: German officers, international crew

Conditions: maximum age 79

Itinerary

Round trip: about 38 days

46 ▼
Hamburg *Germany*	Salonika *Greece*
Rotterdam *Holland*	Istanbul *Turkey*
Valletta *Malta*	Burgas (*on Black Sea, Bulgaria*)
Piraeus *Greece*	Izmir *Turkey*
Heraklion *Crete*	Le Havre *France*
Limassol *Cyprus*	Felixstowe *United Kingdom*
Mersin *Turkey*	Hamburg *Germany*

Ships and Fares

Ulf Ritscher, Widukind

Built in 1990

Round trip: DM5292, or DM140 per day

Hamburg	▶	Piraeus	about 11 days	DM1674
Hamburg	▶	Istanbul	about 22 days	DM3148

Itinerary

Round trip: about 6 to 7 weeks

77 ▼
Hamburg *Germany*	Yanbu *Saudi Arabia*
Rotterdam *Holland*	Jeddah *Saudi Arabia*
Thamesport *United Kingdom*	Port Sudan *Sudan*
Le Havre *France*	Suez *Egypt*
Piraeus *Greece*	Salerno *Italy*
Suez *Egypt*	Valencia *Spain*
Jeddah *Saudi Arabia*	Thamesport *United Kingdom*
Hodeïda *Yemen*	Hamburg *Germany*
Aqaba *Jordan*	

(Passengers cannot go ashore in Saudi Arabia)

Ship and Fares

Red Sea Explorer

Built 1993, 21,000 tons; 8 passengers; 3 twin bedded cabins, 2 single cabins.

Round trip: DM6404/DM7995, or DM136 to DM170 per day

Hamburg	▶	Piraeus		about 12 days	DM1784/DM2180
Hamburg	▶	Red Sea	▶ Salerno	5/6 weeks	DM5348/DM6635

Itinerary

Round trip: about 45 days

78 ▼   Hamburg *Germany*
       Rotterdam *Holland*
       Le Havre *France*
       Piraeus *Greece*
       Suez *Egypt*
       Jeddah *Saudi Arabia*
       Hodeïda *Yemen*
       Aqaba *Jordan*

Jeddah *Saudi Arabia*
Port Sudan *Sudan*
Suez *Egypt*
Salerno *Italy*
Valencia *Spain*
Thamesport *United Kingdom*
Hamburg *Germany*

Ship and Fares

Red Sea Energy

Built in 1986. Formerly the **Ville de Jupiter**
Fare per day: DM130/DM188

Unicorn Lines

King Travel (Pty) Ltd
9th Floor General Building
47 Field Street, PO Box 4690
Durban 4000, South Africa
✆ (31) 304 91 03, ✉ (31) 304 92 00 (international code: 27)

Agent in Germany:

Frachtschiff-Touristik (Captain Peter Zylmann)
Exhöft 12
24404 Maasholm Germany
✆ 0 4642 60 68, ✉ 0 4642 67 67 (international code: 49)

A South African company based in Durban whose ships sail in the Indian Ocean and also in the Mediterranean.

Itinerary

Round trip: about 13 days

156 ▼   Durban *South Africa*
       Cape Town *South Africa*
       Walvis Bay *Namibia*

Cape Town *South Africa*
East London *South Africa*
Durban *South Africa*

Ship and Fares

Sezela, Pongola

> 6 passengers
> Fares: on demand

Itinerary   Round trip: about 49 days

157 ▼ Durban *South Africa*   Bombay *India*
      Nacala *Mozambique*   Mombasa *Kenya*
      Dar es Salaam *Tanzania*   Dar es Salaam *Tanzania*
      Mombasa *Kenya*   Nacala *Mozambique*
      Karachi *Pakistan*   Durban *South Africa*
      Dubai *United Arab Emirates*

Ships and Fares

Tugela, Umgeni

> 10 passengers
> Fares: on demand

United Baltic Corporation

Dexter House
2 Royal Mint Court
London EC3N 4XX United Kingdom
✆ (0171) 265 0808, 🖷 (0171) 481 4784 (international code: 44)

United Baltic Corporation, in the Baltic since 1919, is a division of the British group Andrew Weir Shipping (*see* Bank Line), one of the largest private companies in Great Britain. The **Baltic Eagle** links Holland, England and Belgium to Finland via the Kiel canal or Skaggerak straits. It is possible to stay in Helsinki and wait for the next ship.

Nationalities: British officers and crew
Conditions: maximum age 80

108 ▼ Antwerp *Belgium/*   Hamina *Finland*
        Amsterdam *Holland*   Amsterdam *Holland/*
        Turku *Finland*   Antwerp *Belgium*
        Helsinki *Finland*

Ships and Fares

Baltic Eagle, Eider

12 or 2 passengers

Round trip: Felixstowe–Finland–Belgium (11 days):
Adults: £675/£725. Children (6 to 12): £450/£485
Children under 6: free

Round trip Belgium–Finland–Holland (10 days):
Adults: £625/£685. Children (6 to 12): £420/£460

Round trip: Felixstowe–Holland–Finland–Belgium–Felixstowe (21 days):
£1200/£1250

One-way trips: £300/£350

Cars: £180; motorbikes: £95

Agencies and Useful Addresses

ABC Cruise and Ferry Guide

Reed Travel Group
Church Street, Dunstable
Bedfordshire
LU5 4HB United Kingdom
✆ (01582) 600111, ✇ (01582) 6695230 (international code: 44)

In North America:

500 Plaza Drive
Secaucus
New Jersey 07094 USA
✆ (201) 902 2000, ✇ (201) 902 7989 (international code: 1)

People who wanted to travel by cargo ship a few years ago or board the last of the passenger liners could consult the *ABC Shipping Guide* (a monthly brochure for travel agencies), which was the only publication to give information on the principal itineraries and fares several months ahead, as well as details on shipping companies offering voyages to passengers.

In March 1993 the famous *ABC Shipping Guide*, with its thin telephone directory pages, disappeared, to be replaced by a new edition on glossy paper which only appears four times a year and is called the *ABC Cruise and Ferry Guide*, a title which appears to exclude cargo ships. No doubt encouraged by the cruise boom, this high quality brochure gives over most of its pages to cruise liners, with a detailed inventory of island, river and coastal cruises and even trips on large sailing boats. You can also read accounts written by members of a specialist team which travels regularly on board the 150 main liners of the world and gives an opinion on each.

As the title indicates, ferries comprise the other half of this brochure, and you can find all the information you need (timetables, fares) concerning large or small ferries, all over the world. The 'Cargo Passenger Services' section is still there, sandwiched between liners and ferries, but unfortunately, contrary to the previous edition, the fares, which were such an important part of it, are no longer featured.

This change in policy does not make matters easy for the traveller. However, the brochure is intended essentially for travel agencies; it refers you to specialist agencies if you need practical information on cargo ships. This has undoubtedly come about because nowadays cargo ship agencies have become more visible, publishing their own brochures and offering an increasing number of voyages.

The *ABC Cruise and Ferry Guide* is still full of possibilities and is a faithful reflection of maritime passenger transport and cruises. You will also find some useful tables, maps and efficient indexes which will enable you to find your bearing in the ever-changing world of navigation. The brochure of 350 pages is available from the above UK address, at £42.50 per issue. A subscription (4 issues per year: March, June, September, December) costs £120. The US equivalent, the *ABC Cruise & Ship Line Guide,* costs $48.40 (subscription $194).

The Reed Group publishes numerous travel guides for travel agencies. Whether about boats, trains, hotels or freight, they are essential reference tools.

Le Cargo Club

Librairie Ulysse
26, rue Saint-Louis-en-l'Ile
75004 Paris France
✆ 43 25 17 35, ✇ 43 29 52 10 (international code: 33)

Founded in 1971 by Catherine Domain, the Librarie Ulysse specializes in travel books and maps. It attracts numerous travellers and globe-trotters.

Situated in the heart of Paris on an island in the middle of the Seine, the bookshop is an ideal anchor for the Cargo Club. It provides a meeting space for those who want to exchange information, impressions or tips on cargo ship travel. Meetings take place on the first Wednesday of each month at about 6.30pm. Bring an aperitif drink as your entry fee. What better place to plan a sea voyage than a bookshop?

Ford's Travel Guides

Ford's Travel Guides
19448 Londelius Street
Northridge, California 91324 USA
✆ (818) 701 74 14 (international code: 1)

Ford Travel Guides, based in California, were founded in 1952 and specialize in maritime travel. There is a *Ford's Cruise Guide* for cruises, and even a *Ford's Deck Plan Guide* for travel agents, which describes the decks on the main liners.

Naturally, it is *Ford's Freighter Guide*, on cargo ships, which to us is the most interesting. Published twice a year, this 150-page book with black and white photos and maps offers about a hundred cargo ship voyages and gives the addresses of numerous specialist agencies. The book also includes a section called 'Waterways of the World' on river and coastal cruises, 'Sports and Casual Cruises', and finally a section entitled 'Ferry Travel Worldwide'.

Ford's Freighter Guide costs US$16.50 per issue, $22 for a subscription (two issues per year: May and November). Add $2.50 per issue for overseas postage.

Frachtschiff-Touristik: Captain Peter Zylmann

Exhöft 12
24404 Maasholm Germany
✆ 0 4642 60 68, 🖶 0 4642 67 67 (international code: 49)

Representative in UK:

The Strand Cruise and Travel Centre
Charing Cross Shopping Concourse
The Strand
London WC2N 4HZ United Kingdom
✆ (0171) 836 6363, 🖶 (0171) 497 0078 (international code: 44)

This agency was founded in 1986 by Peter Zylmann, a long-time sea captain. It is situated in a small fishing port, not far from the Kiel canal linking the Baltic to the North Sea, a busy cargo ship route.

Captain Zylmann's agency is expanding; in 1994 it acquired another Hamburg agency, Margis Reiseagentur. The range of voyages in its brochure is broad: from unusual itineraries such as Dieppe–Abidjan, Amsterdam–Cuba and Antwerp–Manaus (on the Amazon), to a slow journey on the South China or Yellow Seas. You will also find—and this is handy for those who want to do a trial run first—lots of short trips to the North Sea, the Baltic Sea or the Mediterranean. It seems that this former captain has succeeded in persuading all sorts of lesser-known shipping companies to accept passengers on board.

Its user-friendly brochure (written in German) is illustrated with photographs and places emphasis on the cheaper voyages. Unfortunately the names of the shipping companies are not mentioned (as is the case with all German agencies), which is frustrating for the traveller, but in order to make this guide as complete as possible Captain Zylmann has agreed to pass over the names of the shipping companies he represents.

Rather than create a heading for each company represented, we have regrouped them under Captain Zylmann.

Itinerary

9 ▼   Antwerp *Belgium*   *possibly*:
      Chester *Pennsylvania USA*   Chester *Pennsylvania USA*
      Richmond *Virginia USA*   Antwerp *Belgium*

      Company: Independent

Ship and Fares

Container ship of 13,500 tons, indoor swimming pool, sauna

One way: DM1986/DM2574, or DM165 to DM215 per day
Round trip (about 4 weeks): DM4542/DM5992

Itinerary

13 ▼   La Spezia *Italy*   Houston *Texas USA*
      Barcelona *Spain*   New Orleans *Louisiana USA*
      Valencia *Spain*   La Spezia *Italy*
      Miami *Florida USA*

      Company: P. R., on board the **Appolonia**

Fares

Round trip (about 35 days): DM2450/DM4480, or DM70 to DM128 per day

La Spezia	▶	Miami	about 15 days	DM1250/DM2120
La Spezia	▶	Houston	about 18 days	DM1430/DM2474
La Spezia	▶	New Orleans	about 20 days	DM1550/DM2710
New Orleans	▶	La Spezia	about 17 days	DM1370/DM2356

Itinerary

16 ▼   Amsterdam *Holland*   Antwerp *Belgium*
      Cuba   Amsterdam *Holland*
      possibly: Mexico

      Company: Neufeld Schiffahrts

Fares

Round trip: DM4855/DM5310, or DM150 to DM165 per day
Amsterdam ▶ Cuba (about 2 weeks)   DM2195/DM2390
(return trip same price: Cuba ▶ Anvers)

Itinerary   One way: about 18 days

23 ▼   Antwerp/Ghent *Belgium*   La Guaira/Maracaïbo *Venezuela*
       Puerto Cabello *Venezuela*

Company: Reederei Nord

Fares

Belgium   ▶   Venezuela   DM1980, or DM110 per day

Itinerary   Round trip: about 7 weeks

27 ▼   Antwerp *Belgium*   Belem *Brazil*
       Santanas (on the Amazon) *Brazil*   Rouen/Honfleur *France*
       Manaus (on the Amazon) *Brazil*   Bremen *Germany*
       Itacoatiara (on the Amazon) *Brazil*

Company: Parten Reederei, on board the **Neptun**

Fares

Round trip: DM5650/DM6211, or DM115 to DM126 per day

Itinerary   Round trip: about 68 days

37 ▼   Hamburg *Germany*   Antofagasta *Chile*
       Antwerp *Belgium*   Arica *Chile*
       Bilbao *Spain*   Guayaquil *Ecuador*
       Panama Canal   Panama Canal
       Iquique *Chile*   Bilbao *Spain*
       Valparaiso *Chile*   Antwerp *Belgium*
       Talcahuano *Chile*   Hamburg *Germany*
       San Antonio *Chile*

Company: Reederei Oltmann

Fares

Round trip: DM8560/DM10274, or DM125 to DM150 per day

Hamburg	▶	Guayaquil	about 23 days	DM3160/DM3735
Hamburg	▶	Callao	about 25 days	DM3400/DM4025
Hamburg	▶	Iquique	about 28 days	DM3760/DM4460
Hamburg	▶	Valparaiso	about 31 days	DM4120/DM4895
Valparaiso	▶	Hamburg	about 38 days	DM4960/DM5910
Arica	▶	Hamburg	about 29 days	DM3880/DM4605
Guayaquil	▶	Hamburg	about 26 days	DM3520/DM4170

Itinerary

Round trip: about 3 weeks

39 ▼ Hamburg *Germany*
Felixstowe *United Kingdom*
Rotterdam *Holland*
Gibraltar
Ceuta (*Spanish territory in
Morocco*)

Melilla (*Spanish territory in
Morocco*)
Cartagena *Spain*
Cadiz *Spain*
Rotterdam *Holland*
Hamburg *Germany*

Company: Oldenburg Portugiesische Dampfschiffs Reederei (O.P.D.R.)

Fares

Round trip: DM2562/DM3024, or DM122 to DM144 per day
Reduced fare for round trips at certain times of year:
DM1869/DM2192, or DM89 to DM104 per day
Reduced fares for one-way tickets at certain times of year:

Europe	▶	Morocco (8/13 days)	DM1493

Itinerary

Round trip: about 4 weeks

41 ▼ Rotterdam *Holland*
Antwerp *Belgium*
Piraeus *Greece*
Salonika *Greece*

Istanbul *Turkey*
Izmir *Turkey*
Rotterdam *Holland*

Company: Reederei Dede

Fares

Round trip: DM3824/DM4534, or DM136 to DM160 per day

Itinerary

Round trip: 11/16 days

55 ▼ A western European port   Boulogne *France*
      Santander/Bilbao *Spain*   Blyth *United Kingdom*
      Antwerp *Belgium*   Dundee *United Kingdom*

Company: Reederei Russ (paper-carrying vessel)

Fares

Round trip: DM1786/DM1968, or DM110 to DM123 per day

Itinerary

Round trip: 10/11 days

57 ▼ Rotterdam *Holland*   Leixoes *Portugal*
      Lisbon *Portugal*   Rotterdam *Holland*

Company: Ramstad Shipping

Fares

Prices vary according to ship:
Ship 'F', round trip: DM1533/DM1698, or DM139 to DM155 per day
Ship 'J', round trip: DM1458/DM1698, or DM132 to DM155 per day

---

Itinerary

Round trip: about 2 weeks

59 ▼ Rotterdam *Holland*   Casablanca *Morocco*
      Antwerp *Belgium*   Rotterdam *Holland*
      Tangier *Morocco*

Company: O.P.D.R.

Fares

Round trip: DM1787, or DM125 per day
One way: DM1147
Reduced fares at certain times of year:
Round trip: DM1325, or DM95 per day

Itinerary

Round trip: about 2 weeks

60 ▼   A western European port   A western European port
        (Bremen/Rotterdam/Antwerp)   (Bremen/Rotterdam/Antwerp)
        Casablanca *Morocco*

    Company: O.P.D.R.

Fares

    Round trip: DM1787, or DM125 per day
    One way: DM1147
    Reduced fares at certain times of year:
    Round trip: DM1325, or DM95 per day

Itinerary

Round trip: about 3 weeks

62 ▼   Hamburg *Germany*   Santa Cruz de Tenerife
        Felixstowe *United Kingdom*   *Canary Islands*
        Rotterdam *Holland*   *possibly*: Casablanca *Morocco*
        Funchal *Madeira*   Cadiz *Spain*
        Las Palmas *Canary Islands*   Hamburg *Germany*

    Company: O.P.D.R.

Fares

    Round trip: DM2583/DM2835, or DM123 to DM135 per day
    Hamburg   ▶   Las Palmas   about 10 days DM1599/DM1755
    Reduced fares at certain times of year

Itinerary

Round trip: about 6 weeks

67 ▼   Hamburg *Germany*   Port Harcourt *Nigeria*
        Rotterdam *Holland*   Douala *Cameroon*
        Antwerp *Belgium*   Takoradi *Ghana*
        Le Havre *France*   Rotterdam *Holland*
        Tema *Ghana*   Teesport *United Kingdom*
        Cotonou *Benin*   Hamburg *Germany*
        Lagos *Nigeria*

    Company: Kaiama

Fares

Round trip: DM7285/DM7999, or DM173 to DM190 per day
Hamburg   ▶   Douala   about 23 days   DM4055/DM4446

Itinerary

Round trip: about 3 weeks

68 ▼   Dieppe *France*   Dieppe *France*
       Abidjan *Ivory Coast*

Company: Vega Dania Line

Fares

Round trip: DM1964/DM2678, or DM93 to DM127 per day
One way: DM1300/DM1410

Itinerary

Round trip: 8/9 weeks

80 ▼   Hamburg *Germany*   Tanga *Tanzania*
       Antwerp *Belgium*   Mombasa *Kenya*
       Fos-sur-mer *France*   *possibly*: Djibouti *and* Port Sudan
       Suez Canal   Suez Canal
       possibly: Port Sudan *Sudan*   Le Havre *France*
       Djibouti   Felixstowe *United Kingdom*
       Dar es Salaam *Tanzania*   Hamburg *Germany*

Company: Caledonia Schiffahrts ges

Fares

Round trip: DM7038/DM7638, or DM110 to DM120 per day

Fos-sur-mer	▶	Mombasa	about 21 days	DM2592/DM2802
Mombasa	▶	Hamburg	about 21 days	DM2706/DM2926
Hamburg	▶	Dar es Salaam	about 28 days	DM3276/DM3546

Itinerary

82 ▼ Hamburg *Germany*   Bombay *India*
       Felixstowe *United Kingdom*   Colombo *Sri Lanka*
       Rotterdam *Holland*   Karachi *Pakistan*
       Suez Canal   Suez Canal
       Fujairah *United Arab Emirates*   Hamburg *Germany*
       Karachi *Pakistan*

Company: Reederei Nord

Fares

Round trip: DM8110/DM8905, or DM128 to DM140 per day

Hamburg	▶	Karachi	about 23 days	DM3610/DM3955
Return trip the same price				
Hamburg	▶	Bombay	about 28 days	DM4360/DM4780
Return trip the same price				
Hamburg	▶	Colombo	about 33 days	DM5110/DM5605
Colombo	▶	Hamburg	about 25 days	DM3910/DM4285

Itinerary

85 ▼ Bremen *Germany*   Hong Kong
       Southampton *United Kingdom*   Singapore
       Algeciras *Spain*   Colombo *Sri Lanka*
       Suez Canal   Suez Canal
       Jeddah *Saudi Arabia*   Algeciras *Spain*
       Dubai *United Arab Emirates*   Southampton *United Kingdom*
       Hong Kong   Rotterdam *Holland*
       Pusan *South Korea*   Bremen *Germany*
       Kaohsiung *Taiwan*

Fares

Round trip: DM7998/DM12,445, or DM123 to DM191 per day

Algeciras	▶	Algeciras	about 52 days	DM6465/DM9974
Bremen	▶	Hong Kong	about 28 days	DM3560/DM5489
Singapore	▶	Bremen	about 23 days	DM2985/DM4549

Itinerary

Round trip: about 120 days

89 ▼ A western European port
Antwerp *Belgium*
Casablanca *Morocco*
Various Mediterranean ports,
amongst them:
   Marseilles *France*
   Genoa *Italy*
   Naples *Italy*
   La Goulette *Tunisia*
   or
   Constanza *Romania (Black Sea)*
Suez Canal
Singapore
Hong Kong

Various Chinese ports on the
Yellow Sea, amongst them:
   Shanghai
   Huangpu
   Lianyungang
   Qingdao
   Tianjin
   Quinghuangdao
   Dalian
possibly: Pusan *South Korea*
Huangnam *North Korea*
Chungjin *North Korea*
*(return journey via the
Mediterranean)*
A western European port

Company: C-P Line

Fares

Round trip: DM9856, or DM82 per day

Itinerary

Round trip: 11/16 days

105 ▼ A western European port
   Kotka *Finland*
   Hamina *Finland*
   Hanko *Finland*

Rauma *Finland*
Oulu *Finland*
A western European port

Company: Reederei Russ

Fares

Round trip: DM1786/DM1968, or DM124 per day

Itinerary Round trip: about 1 week

106 ▼ Hamburg *Germany*
    Ports in Norway
      (Oslo, Moss, Kristiansand)
    Ports in Sweden
      (Gothenburg, Halmstadt,
      Stockholm, Gävle, Norrköping,
      Karlshamn)

Ports in Finland
  (Helsinki, Hanko, Rauma,
  Turku, Mäntilouto)
Ports in Poland:
  (Gdynia, Szczecin)
Ports in Belgium
  (Antwerp, Zeebrugge)
Hamburg *Germany*

Company: Mathias Schiffahrts

Fares

Round trip: DM980, or DM140 per day

Itinerary Round trip: 6/8 days

107 ▼ Hamburg *Germany*
    Kiel Canal
    Sweden
    Finland

Norway
Kiel Canal
Hamburg *Germany*

Company: Parten Reederei, on board the **Coronel**

Fares

Round trip: DM980, or DM123 per day

Itinerary Round trip: about 2 weeks

109 ▼ Emden *Germany*
    Helgoland Islands *Germany*
    Kiel Canal
    Fredericia *Denmark*
    Horsens *Denmark*
    Køge *Denmark*

Ports in Finland:
  (Helsinki, Kotka, Hamina,
  Saimaaseen)
Vyborg *Russia*
A port in Germany

Company: Herbert Meyer Schiffahrts K.G.

Fares

Round trip: DM1682, or DM130 per day

Itinerary

Round trip: about 14 days

113 ▼ Rotterdam *Holland*
Kiel Canal
Helsinki *Finland*
St Petersburg *Russia*
Helsinki *Finland*

possibly: Aarhus *Denmark*
Kiel Canal
Bremen *Germany*
Rotterdam *Holland*

Company: Reederei Ritscher

Fares

Round trip: DM1597/DM2171, or DM114 to DM155 per day

Itinerary

Round trip: 10/12 days

114 ▼ Kiel *Germany*
Antwerp *Belgium*
Kiel *Germany*

Skölvig *Finland*
Kiel *Germany*

Company: North Navigation

Fares

Round trip: DM1526, or DM127 per day

Itinerary

Round trip: 6/7 days

116 ▼ Hamburg *Germany*
Bremen *Germany*
possibly: Oslo *Norway*
Gothenburg *Sweden*
Copenhagen *Denmark*

Malmö *Sweden*
Helsingborg *Sweden*
Kiel Canal
Hamburg *Germany*

Company: K.G. Schiffahrts ges Beutelrock

Fares

Round trip: DM980, or DM140 per day

Itinerary

117 ▼ Hamburg *Germany*   Copenhagen *Denmark*
  Kiel Canal   *or* Helsinborg *Sweden*
  Copenhagen *Denmark* *or* Malmö *Sweden*
  or Helsinborg *Sweden* Kiel Canal
  or Malmö *Sweden*   Bremen *Germany*
  Gothenburg *Sweden* Hamburg *Germany*

  Company: J. Kahrs K.G.

Fares

Round trip DM980, or DM140 per day

Itinerary

118 ▼ Hamburg *Germany*   Aarhus *Denmark*
  Bremen *Germany*   Ports in Denmark or Sweden
  Oslo *Norway*   Kiel Canal
  or Gothenburg *Sweden* Hamburg *Germany*

  Company: Reederei Speck

Fares

Round trip: DM980, or DM140 per day

Itinerary

119 ▼ Kiel *Germany*   *ports of call on the Mälaren*
  Goole (River Humber) *Sea, occasionally as far as*
   United Kingdom   Västeras *Sweden*
  A port in Sweden, *with various* Kiel *Germany*

Fares

Round trip: DM1898, or DM135 per day

Itinerary

120 ▼ Hamburg *Germany*
Kiel Canal
Gdynia *Poland*

Kiel Canal
Bremen *Germany*
Hamburg *Germany*

Company: Mathias Schiffahrts

Fares

Round trip: DM980, or DM140 per day

Itinerary

Round trip: about 2 weeks

122 ▼ Kiel *Germany*
Aarhus *Denmark*
Riga *Latvia*
Kiel Canal

Tilbury *United Kingdom*
possibly: Rotterdam *Holland*
or Antwerp *Belgium*
Kiel *Germany*

Company: West Navigation Company

Fares

Round trip: DM1772, or DM126 per day

Itinerary

Round trip: about 2 weeks

123 ▼ Hamburg/Stadersand *Germany*
Rotterdam *Holland*
Dublin *Ireland*
Belfast *Northern Ireland*
Cork *Ireland*

Southampton *United Kingdom*
Le Havre *France*
Antwerp *Belgium*
Hamburg *Germany*

Company: Reederei U. Salge

Fares

Round trip: DM1896/DM2192, or DM135 to DM156 per day

Itinerary

124 ▼   Antwerp *Belgium*   Le Havre *France*
       Dublin *Ireland*   Antwerp *Belgium*

       Company: Caribic Navigation

Fares

Round trip: DM980, or DM140 per day

Itinerary

125 ▼   Le Havre *France*   Greenock *United Kingdom*
       Southampton *United Kingdom*   Southampton *United Kingdom*
       Dublin *Ireland*   Le Havre *France*
       Belfast *Northern Ireland*

       Company: Reederei Uwe Jess

Fares

Round trip: DM980, or DM140 per day

Itinerary

137 ▼   Miami *Florida USA*   La Guaira *Venezuela*
       Aruba *Curaçao*   Miami *Florida USA*
       Puerto Cabello *Venezuela*

       Company: Schiffahrts Oltmann

Fares

Round trip: DM2104, or DM175 per day

Freighter Cruise Service

Suite 103, 5925 Monkland Avenue
Montreal
Quebec H4A 1G7 Canada
✆ (514) 481 04 47 (international code: 1)

Freighter Cruise Service is one of the oldest agencies specializing in cargo ships, as it was created in 1956 after an unforgettable journey. Mrs Geraldine Simpson, a woman of some character, ran a tea room and a shop in Quebec. Having decided to travel to Egypt, she chose to go by cargo ship to take maximum advantage of the numerous ports of call which would enable her to buy things for her shop.

While making her reservation, she discovered that she was the only tourist on board, even though there were 50 places available on the ship. Acting as a travel agent, Geraldine Simpson quickly managed to sell the other 49 places in three weeks. She had found her vocation. Unfortunately, she forgot to take into account certain unknown factors like world conflicts: the Suez Crisis had erupted. Only nine passengers didn't cancel. Mrs Simpson had a memorable trip in the Mediterranean despite this, and it changed the course of her life. Realizing that there was a real demand for travel by cargo ship, she decided to found a specialist agency as soon as she returned to Montreal.

During her life, Mrs Simpson had the opportunity to travel all round the world by cargo ship. Today her daughter, Mary Simpson, is running the agency. Their brochure offers about 50 voyages worldwide. Freighter Cruise Service's motto is 'You have the time. We have the ships.'

Freighter World Cruises

180 South Lake Avenue #335
Pasadena
California 91101 USA
✆ (818) 449 31 06, ✆ (818) 449 95 73 (international code: 1)

This agency, based in California, has specialized in travel by cargo ship since 1977. It represents about 15 shipping companies and serves as an intermediary between passengers and the companies that handle their own reservations.

In order to get itself better known and to offer various trips, this agency— which calls itself 'the largest travel agency in the world dedicated to freighter travel'—publishes a unique fortnightly report, illustrated with black and white photos. *Freighter Space Advisory* is distributed to former clients or on subscription. This user-friendly publication offers immediate departures at reduced prices, and a whole series of voyages to the four corners of the earth, usually departing from the USA. You can find out more by telephoning Margi, Joycene or Lyn, who have all sailed in cargo ships. Annual subscription: US$33.

Furthermore, Freighter World Cruises publishes travellers' personal accounts to give you an idea of what to expect before you leave.

Itinerary

Round trip: 35/37 days

138 ▼ Savannah *Georgia USA*
    Fernandina Beach *Florida USA*
    Santos *Brazil*
    Buenos Aires *Argentina*
    Montevideo *Uruguay*

Rio Grande *Brazil*
Santos *Brazil*
possibly: Vitoria *Brazil*
Norfolk *Virginia USA*

Company: Reederei Bernhard Schulte

Ship and Fares

Alabama

Container ship built in 1991, 4 passengers (2 double cabins)
Round trip: $3125, or $85 per day

Itinerary

Round trip: about 21 days

140 ▼ Long Beach *California USA*
    Puerto Quetzal *Guatemala*
    Balboa *Panama*

Puerto Caldera *Costa Rica*
Acajutla *Salvador*
Long Beach *California USA*

Company: Kahrs Line

Ship and Fares

Maya Tikal

9500 tons, 5 passengers
Round trip: $1660/$1770, or $79 to $84 per day

Hamburg-Süd

Hamburg-Süd Reiseagentur
Ost-West Str. 59–61
20457 Hamburg Germany
✆ (040) 37 05 155, 📠 (040) 37 05 24 20 (international code: 49)

This large shipping company was founded in 1871 under the name 'Hamburg-Südamerikanische', as it had links with South America. During the 1930s it even had a liner, the **Cap Arcona**, sailing on this route.

Hamburg-Süd (its proper name is Hamburg-Sudamerikanische Dampschiffahrts Gesellschaft, or H.S.D.G.) is both a shipping company and a travel agency specializing in cargo ships since 1950. You will not be able to board ships bearing the company name, although a subsidiary of the company, Columbus Line (in operation since 1957), takes passengers on board.

The Hamburg-Süd agency offers numerous worldwide voyages on board cargo ships belonging to other companies, many departuring from Germany.

Itinerary

Round trip: about 30 days

47 ▼ Rotterdam *Holland*
      Gibraltar
      Piraeus *Greece*
      Limassol *Cyprus*
      Alexandria *Egypt*
      Ashdod *Israel*
      Haifa *Israel*

Tartus *Syria*
Izmir *Turkey*
Salerno *Italy*
Gibraltar
Tilbury *United Kingdom*
Antwerp *Belgium*
Rotterdam *Holland*

Fares

Round trip: DM3880/DM4 750, or DM129 to DM158 per day

Itinerary

Round trip: about 4 weeks

48 ▼ Hamburg *Germany*   Ashdod *Israel*
       Bremen *Germany*   Haifa *Israel*
       Rotterdam *Holland*   Bremen *Germany*
       Limassol *Cyprus*   Hamburg *Germany*

Company: Interorient

Ship and Fares

Nautique

Built in 1993

Round trip: DM3625/DM4 750, or DM129 to DM169 per day
Germany   ▶   Israel   about 12 days   DM1432/DM2100

Itinerary

Round trip: about 33 days

51 ▼ Hamburg *Germany*   Tartus *Syria*
       Rotterdam *Holland*   Lattakia *Syria*
       Antwerp *Belgium*   Mersin/Izmir *Turkey*
       Malta   Salerno *Italy*
       Alexandria *Egypt*   Felixstowe *United Kingdom*
       Beirut *Lebanon*   Hamburg *Germany*

Fares

Round trip: DM3840/DM5160, or DM116 to DM156 per day

Itinerary

Round trip: 7/12 days

115 ▼ A port in Germany   Denmark
        Sweden   A port in Germany

Fares

Round trip: 990 DM/1300 DM

Itinerary   Round trip: about 7 days

126 ▼   Rotterdam *Holland*   Belfast *Northern Ireland*
        Cork *Ireland*   Rotterdam *Holland*
        Dublin *Ireland*

Fares

Round trip: DM910/DM1390, or DM130 to DM198 per day

Hamburger Abendblatt/Die Welt

Verkaufsburö/Seetouristik
Große Bleichen 68
20354 Hamburg Germany
✆ (040) 347 2 49 17, 🖷 (040) 35 27 96 (international code: 49)

This agency specializing in travel by cargo ship was set up in 1994 by Anke
Homann, a well known figure amongst cargo ship travellers, as for many years
she ran another cargo ship agency, Margis, now owned by Captain Zylmann. It
was set up in Hamburg in association with two newspapers, the *Hamburger
Abendblatt* and the daily *Die Welt*, and a travel agency with numerous offices,
First Reiseburo. It offers about 60 voyages worldwide.

Like all other agencies in Germany, the names of the shipping companies are
not mentioned in the description of the voyages.

Itinerary   Round trip: 62/67 days

17 ▼   Hamburg *Germany*   Quetzal *Guatemala*
        Bremen *Germany*   Corinto *Nicaragua*
        Antwerp *Belgium*   Buenaventura *Colombia*
        Rio Haina *Dominican Republic* San Lorenzo *Ecuador*
        Cartagena *Colombia*   Panama Canal
        Panama Canal   Bremen *Germany*
        Caldera *Costa Rica*   Hamburg *Germany*
        Acajutla *San Salvador*

Fares

Round trip: DM6030, or DM90 per day

| Europe | ▶ | Cartagena | about 26 days | DM2340 |
| Europe | ▶ | Acajutla | about 42 days | DM3780 |

Itinerary

Round trip: about 44 days

25 ▼

Bremen *Germany*	Willemstad *Curaçao*
Rotterdam *Holland*	Oranjestad *Aruba*
Felixstowe *United Kingdom*	Cartagena *Colombia*
Paramaribo *Surinam*	Puerto Cabello *Venezuela*
Georgetown *Guyana*	Guanta *Venezuela*
Port of Spain *Trinidad*	Rotterdam *Holland*
La Guaira *Venezuela*	Bremen *Germany*

Fares

Round trip: DM4 840, or DM110 per day

Europe	▶	Paramaribo	about 14 days	DM1540
Europe	▶	Georgetown	about 16 days	DM1760
Europe	▶	Port of Spain	about 19 days	DM2090
Europe	▶	La Guaira	about 20 days	DM2200
Europe	▶	Willemstad	about 21 days	DM2310
Europe	▶	Oranjestad	about 22 days	DM2420
Europe	▶	Cartagena	about 24 days	DM2640

Itinerary

Round trip: 42/45 days

26 ▼

Sète *France*	Degrad des Cannes *French Guyana*
or Valencia *Spain*	Belem *Brazil*
Marina di Carrara *Italy*	Valencia *Spain*
Marseilles *France*	*or* Sète *France*
Banjul *Gambia*	

Company: Hartmann Schiffahrts

Ships and Fares
Delmas Kourou, Delmas Montjoly

8985 tons

Round trip: DM5460/DM5625, or DM121 to DM125 per day

| Europe | ▶ | Guyana | about 21 days | DM2625 |

Itinerary

Round trip: about 27 days

43 ▼ Rotterdam *Holland*   Piraeus *Greece*
     Tilbury *United Kingdom*   Felixstowe *United Kingdom*
     Piraeus *Greece*   Rotterdam *Holland*
     Izmir *Turkey*

Fares

Round trip: DM3321/DM3625, or DM123 to DM134 per day

Itinerary

Round trip: about 33 days

50 ▼ Hamburg/Bremen *Germany*   Tartus *Syria*
     Rotterdam *Holland*   Lattakia *Syria*
     Antwerp *Belgium*   Mersin/Izmir *Turkey*
     Alexandria *Egypt*   Salerno *Italy*
     Port Said *Egypt*   Felixstowe *United Kingdom*
     Beirut *Lebanon*   Hamburg/Bremen *Germany*

Fares

Round trip: DM4290/DM5160, or DM130 to DM156 per day

Or, in a different boat with an almost identical itinerary:
Round trip (about 32 days): DM3600, or DM112 per day

Itinerary

Round trip: about 1 week

54 ▼ Rotterdam *Holland*   Le Havre *France*
     Santurce/Bilbao *Spain*   Rotterdam *Holland*

Fares

Round trip: DM945, or DM135 per day

Itinerary

56 ▼   Rotterdam *Holland*   Leixoes *Portugal*
         Lisbon *Portugal*   Lisbon *Portugal*
         Leixoes *Portugal*   Vigo *Spain*
         Vigo *Spain*   Le Havre *France*
         Le Havre *France*   Rotterdam *Holland*
         Antwerp *Belgium*

Fares

Round trip: DM1290/DM1540, or DM117 to DM140 per day

Itinerary

58 ▼   Rotterdam *Holland*   Casablanca *Morocco*
         Antwerp *Belgium*   Cadiz *Spain*
         Tangier *Morocco*   Felixstowe *United Kingdom*
         Gibraltar   Rotterdam *Holland*
         Cadiz *Spain*

Fares

Round trip: DM2430, or DM135 per day
Rotterdam   ▶   Casablanca/Cadiz   about 10 days   DM1350

Itinerary

61 ▼   Bremen *Germany*   Antwerp *Belgium*
         Antwerp *Belgium*   Tangier *Morocco*
         Casablanca *Morocco*   Casablanca *Morocco*
         Bremen *Germany*/   Rotterdam *Holland*
            Rotterdam *Holland*

Fares

Round trip: DM1526, or DM138 per day

Itinerary

Round trip: about 6 weeks

65 ▼ Hamburg *Germany*
Rotterdam *Holland*
Antwerp *Belgium*
Le Havre *France*
possibly: Las Palmas *Canary
Islands*
Tema *Ghana*

Cotonou *Benin*
Port Harcourt *Nigeria*
Douala *Cameroon*
Takoradi *Ghana*
Rotterdam *Holland*
Teesport *United Kingdom*
Hamburg *Germany*

Fares

Round trip: DM5670, or DM135 per day

Hamburg	▶	Tema	DM1890
Hamburg	▶	Douala	DM2565

Itinerary

Round trip: about 84 days

102 ▼ Salerno *Italy*
La Spezia *Italy*
Fos-sur-Mer *France*
Barcelona *Spain*
Piraeus *Greece*
Suez Canal
Jeddah *Saudi Arabia*
Fremantle *Australia*
Melbourne *Australia*
Sydney *Australia*
Auckland *New Zealand*

Wellington *New Zealand*
Port Chalmers *New Zealand*
Melbourne *Australia*
Fremantle *Australia*
Jeddah *Saudi Arabia*
Suez Canal
Piraeus *Greece*
Barcelona *Spain*
Fos-sur-mer *France*
La Spezia *Italy*
Salerno *Italy*

Fares

Round trip: DM11,760/DM12,600, or DM140 to DM150 per day

Itinerary
Round trip: 6/7 days

111 ▼ Bremen *Germany*
　　　 Aarhus *Denmark*
　　　 Gothenburg *Sweden*
　　　 Helsinborg *Sweden*
　　　 Malmö *Sweden*

or Hamburg *Germany*
Kiel Canal
Helsinki *Finland*
Kotka *Finland*
A port in *Germany*

Fares

Round trip: DM945/DM1050, or DM135 to DM150 per day

Itinerary

Round trip: about 8 days

112 ▼ Rotterdam *Holland*
　　　 (*via the Skagerrak Straits*)
　　　 Helsinki *Finland*

Teesport *United Kingdom*
Rotterdam *Holland*

Fares

Round trip: DM1150/DM1390, or DM143 to DM173 per day

Mer et Voyages

Mer et Voyages
3, rue Tronchet
75008 Paris France
✆ (1) 44 51 01 68, 🖷 (1) 40 07 12 72 (international code: 33)

This maritime agency was set up in 1994 by cruise and tourism professionals. Its 'travel by cargo ship' department was set up as a result of this guidebook. It is the first French agency to specialize in cargo ships, and it offers trips to the four corners of the earth, on comfortable tramp steamers, luxurious banana boats or on the brand new French oceanographic vessel, the **Marion Dufresne**, fitted as a passenger-cargo ship, sailing around the Kerguelen islands in the South Seas.

As agent to several shipping companies, Mer et Voyages offers sailings at short notice for those who are not particular about their destination. It also offers sailings on more regular routes, whether to North or South America, the Caribbean, the Pacific, the Mediterranean, Africa or the Far East.

Ships Monthly

Waterway Productions
Kottingham House
Dale Street
Burton-on-Trent DE14 3TD United Kingdom
✆ (01283) 56 42 90, 🖷 (01283) 56 10 77 (international code: 44)

This little monthly magazine, popular with ship lovers, publishes extensive information and current and old photographs on all types of vessel: cargo ships, liners, ferries, study ships and war ships. It calls itself 'the international magazine for ship lovers, ashore and afloat.' From time to time the magazine publishes in-depth articles, practical facts and sometimes quirky information on travelling by cargo ship.

One year's subscription is £21.60 in the UK and £29.50 abroad.

Strand Cruise and Travel Centre

Charing Cross Shopping Concourse
The Strand
London WC2N 4HZ United Kingdom
✆ (0171) 836 63 63, 🖷 (0171) 497 00 78 (international code: 44)

This agency was established in 1987 and is based in the heart of London. The passenger cargo ship department was set up by John Alton. Strand publish an informative and colourful brochure, the only one of its kind. More than 30 shipping companies are represented, offering a very wide range of voyages worldwide.

Strand also offer all sorts of travel options: holidays, hotel rooms or excursions in various countries, as well as air/sea ticket combinations for those who only want to travel one way by ship.

Trav'l Tips

Cruise & Freighter Travel Association
Department V5
Post Office Box 218
Flushing N Y 11358 USA
✆ (800) 872 85 84 (international code: 1)

This agency has been specializing in unusual maritime voyages since 1967. It offers all types of voyage—cargo ships, expeditionary vessels, positional cruises on liners—and publishes travellers' personal experiences, as well as a brochure of 32 pages periodically updated for cargo ships.

If you become a member, you will receive their publication *Roam the World by Freighter*, reduced fares and opportunities to travel on a large number of vessels. The cost of becoming a member is US$15 per year or $25 for two years, plus overseas postage.

Other Agencies

In the UK:

Cargo Ship Voyages
5 Hemley Hall Road
Hemley
Woodbridge
Suffolk IP 12 4QF United Kingdom
✆ (01473) 73 62 65, ✆ (01473) 21 15 06 (international code: 44)

Gdynia America Shipping Lines
Passenger Department
238 City Road
London EC1V 2QL United Kingdom
✆ (0171) 251 33 89, ✆ (0171) 250 36 25 (international code: 44)

Representatives in the UK for Polish Ocean Lines and N.S.B.

Gill's Travel
23 Heol-Y-Deri
Rhiwbina
Cardiff CF4 6YF United Kingdom
✆ (01222) 69 38 08 (international code: 44)

This independent travel agency, created in 1957, specializes in travel by cargo ship. You can obtain information from Mike Davies, who has many years' maritime experience.

In Switzerland:

Wagner Frachtschiffreisen
Stradlerstr. 48
CH–8404 Winterthur Switzerland
✆ (052) 242 14 42, ✇ (052) 242 14 87 (international code: 41)

In the USA:

Anytime Anywhere Travel
91 North Bedford Road
Chappaqua, NY 10514 USA
✆ (914) 238 88 00 (international code: 1)

Cargo ship specialists since 1943.

CDP Travel
5 Third Street, Suite 820
San Francisco
California 94103 USA
✆ (415) 882 44 90
or: (800) 886 44 90 (international code: 1)

Pearl's Travel Tips
9903 Oaks Lane
Seminole
Florida 34642 USA
✆ (813) 393 29 19, ✇ (813) 392 25 80 (international code: 1)

In Canada:

Hagen's Travel
320–1425 Marine Drive
West Vancouver
British Columbia V7T 1B9 Canada
✆ (604) 926 43 04 (international code: 1)

The Cruise People
1252 Lawrence Avenue E. # 202
Don Mills
Ontario M3A 1C3 Canada
✆ (416) 444 24 10
or: (800) 268 65 23, ✇ (416) 447 26 28 (international code: 1)

Conrad, Joseph, *Lord Jim* (1890); *The Heart of Darkness* (1902); *Youth* (1902); *Typhoon* (1903); *The Mirror of the Sea* (1906); *The Arrow of Gold* (short story) (1919)

Hergé, *The Crab with the Golden Claws, The Shooting Star, The Red Sea Sharks, Red Rackham's Treasure, Land of Black Gold* (Methuen)

Kerouac, Jack, *Lonesome Traveller* (André Deutsch, 1960)

Lowry, Malcolm, *Ultramarine* (Jonathan Cape, 1933)

Maxtone-Graham, John, *The Only Way to Cross* (Patrick Stephen, 1983); *Crossing and Cruising* (Scribners, New York, 1992)

Mutis, Alvaro, *The Tramp Steamer's Last Call* (Picador, 1993)

Young, Gavin, *Slow Boats to China* (Hutchinson/Penguin, 1981); *Slow Boats Home* (Hutchinson/Penguin, 1985)

Further Reading

Index of Ports